SOPHIE KAY'S

CASSEROLES
AND
ONE·DISH
M·E·A·L·S

ideals®

Ideals Publishing Corp.
Nashville, Tennessee

Contents

One-Dish Meal Basics 4

Homestyle 6

Meatless. 11

Meat 15

Eggs & Cheese. 22

Brunch 28

Skillet 33

Leftovers 40

Low Calorie. 45

Fish & Seafood 49

International 53

Entertaining 59

Index. 64

This cookbook is one of a series of limited edition hardcover cookbooks. Other books in the series include:

Budget Saving Meals Cookbook   Low Calorie Cookbook
Chicken and Poultry Cookbook   Lunch and Brunch Cookbook
Grill and Barbecue Cooking   Old-Fashioned Family Cookbook
Ground Meat Cookbook   Soup, Salad and Sandwich Cookbook
Guide to Microwave Cookbook   Wok Cookbook
Hershey's ® Chocolate and Cocoa Cookbook

For more information on and a full description of any of the Ideals cookbooks listed above, please write:
    Ideals Cookbooks
    P.O. Box 148000
    Nashville, TN 37214-8000

Published by Ideals Publishing Corporation
Nashville, TN 37214
Published simultaneously in Canada

Cover recipe:
German-Style Salad with
Frankfurters, page 18

Mexi-Grande Pie, page 6

One-Dish Meal Basics

One-dish meals, casseroles, skillet dishes, or call it what you will, can be easy on the budget, good tasting and easy to prepare. Casseroles can be everything from hearty and wholesome for the family to elegant and attractive for company. Casseroles can be made from scratch or from planaheads or planned-overs, modern-day words for leftovers or food extended from one meal to another.

Oven casserole dishes can save energy. Check a dish's progress by looking through the oven window instead of opening and closing the oven, causing precious heat loss. Save energy also by making two casseroles at one time. Bake and serve one to the family and freeze the other for later use.

Most one-dish casserole dishes do not need to be cooked in a preheated oven. Soufflés or casseroles that include leavening agents should be baked in a preheated oven.

FREEZING

Most casseroles freeze well. After baking a casserole, cool it quickly by putting it in the sink or in a very large bowl filled with cold water and ice. Then wrap tightly and freeze.

Unbaked casseroles also can be frozen. Line the casserole dish with foil, fill the dish and cover tightly with foil. Freeze until solid. Then remove the frozen casserole from the dish and return to the freezer. The food will retain the shape of the dish which will be used again later for baking.

Most casseroles can be frozen for 1 to 3 months. To thaw, let the casserole thaw in the refrigerator. Then it will thaw and reheat evenly.

Cooked foods such as chili con carne, chop suey, baked beans and pizza freeze satisfactorily. Be sure to pack them in airtight containers or wrap tightly, then freeze immediately.

Uncooked foods that have been frozen and then thawed should be cooked immediately. The cooked food may then be frozen if desired, but *never* thaw and refreeze uncooked foods.

Undersalt or underseason casseroles that are to be frozen. Some flavors become stronger and others tend to fade after freezing. Garlic, pepper and clove become stronger after freezing, while onion, salt and sage become milder or fade almost completely.

Always add crumb and cheese toppings to frozen food just before baking.

A rich flaky pastry topping added to a meat or vegetable stew results in a delicious one-dish meal. The unbaked pastry topping may be added before freezing, or it may be made fresh and placed on the frozen pie when it is baked or heated before serving.

Always buy the best airtight and moisture-proof wrapping materials to retain the most flavor in the product when it is frozen. Some wrapping materials have two layers. One layer is usually paper, and the other is a plastic or waxed coating. The plastic or waxed side should always be placed next to the product to be frozen. Avoid wrapping materials that tear easily or stick to frozen food, such as wax paper or butcher paper. Always label and date each package before freezing.

TIMELY TIPS

Good ingredients make for a good-tasting casserole, but you can save money by selecting food appropriate for a specific use. For example, canned tomatoes that will be used for a casserole do not have to be fancy or the most expensive brand. The shape of a tomato is not important when it is to be used in most casseroles so don't pay the extra cost. Grated tuna costs less than chunk-style, but the flavor is the same in a casserole.

SUBSTITUTIONS

When substituting frozen vegetables for fresh, remember it generally takes less time to cook frozen vegetables. The blanching process used before freezing vegetables precooks them, thereby decreasing the cooking time.

CASSEROLES WITH PASTA

Pasta to be used in casseroles should be undercooked by one-third of the boiling time specified in package directions. Casseroles with pasta can be stored in the refrigerator 1 to 2 days. To bake refrigerated casseroles, allow 15 to 20 minutes extra baking time. To reheat, add a few tablespoons of water, broth or tomato juice to the casserole, if needed. Then cover and heat in a 350° oven until the center is hot and bubbly.

CASSEROLE VARIETIES

Pasta or Cereal	Meat	Vegetable	Soup	Topping
3 cups cooked rice	2 4½-ounce cans shrimp, rinsed and drained	1 cup cooked peas or lima beans ⅓ cup sliced black olives	10¾-ounce can condensed cream of shrimp soup	½ cup toasted slivered almonds or chopped nuts
3 cups cooked noodles	2 cups cubed cooked beef, chicken, turkey or ham	1 cup cooked corn or green beans or lima beans or peas	10¾-ounce can condensed cream of celery soup	1 cup crushed corn chips, potato chips, French-fried onion rings or ½ cup grated Cheddar cheese
3 cups cooked macaroni	2 7-ounce cans tuna or salmon, drained	1 cup cooked peas or green beans or lima beans or ½ cup vegetables and ½ cup mandarin oranges	10¾-ounce can condensed cream of mushroom soup or Cheddar cheese soup	1 cup chow mein noodles or ½ cup toasted wheat germ
3 cups quick-cooking rice	2 cups cubed chicken or turkey	1 cup cooked peas ⅓ cup sliced pimento-stuffed olives	10¾-ounce can condensed cream of chicken soup plus ¾ cup grated Cheddar or American cheese	½ cup buttered bread crumbs

TO ASSEMBLE CASSEROLE: Combine meat, cereal and vegetables. Mix soup with ½ cup milk or plain yogurt. Add to meat mixture; mix lightly. Place in greased 1-quart casserole. Add topping; bake in preheated 375° oven about 25 to 30 minutes or until hot and bubbly. Makes 4 to 6 servings.

Homestyle

Mexi-Grande Pie

Makes 6 to 8 servings
Preparation Time: 25 minutes; 1 hour to bake

    2 pounds lean ground beef
 1½ cups medium-fine cracker crumbs
    2 eggs, lightly beaten
    1 16-ounce can tomato sauce
    2 tablespoons instant onion flakes
    2 teaspoons salt
  ½ teaspoon chili powder
  ¼ teaspoon garlic powder
  ⅛ teaspoon cayenne pepper
    1 8-ounce can whole kernel corn, drained
    1 10-ounce package frozen carrots and peas, thawed
    1 cup shredded process American cheese, lightly packed
    3 cups mashed potatoes
    1 tablespoon butter, melted
      Paprika

Preheat oven to 350°. Mix beef, cracker crumbs, eggs, 1 cup tomato sauce, onion flakes, salt, chili powder, garlic powder and cayenne pepper in bowl. Press into 2-quart round casserole dish, building up sides to form well in center. Bake 25 minutes. Arrange vegetables in center of pie. Top with remaining 1 cup tomato sauce. Bake 20 minutes. Sprinkle cheese over vegetables. Top meat with 6 ½-cup scoops of mashed poatoes. Drizzle butter over potatoes; sprinkle with paprika. Bake 10 minutes.

Chicken Napoli

Makes 4 servings
Preparation Time: 40 minutes

    2 large whole chicken breasts, halved
    1 teaspoon salt
  ½ teaspoon dried basil
  ¼ teaspoon ground black pepper
    3 tablespoons butter
    1 teaspoon vegetable oil
    2 cups water
  ½ cup tomato sauce
    3 cups mostaccioli or macaroni
    2 cups broccoli flowerets, cooked
    2 tablespoons flour
    1 cup milk

Rub chicken breasts with ½ teaspoon salt mixed with basil and pepper. Brown in 1 tablespoon butter and oil in 10-inch skillet over low heat, about 10 minutes on each side. Mix water and tomato sauce in saucepan; bring to boil. Pour over chicken. Stir in mostaccioli; return to boil. Cook, uncovered, 10 minutes. Arrange broccoli around edge of skillet to form border. Heat about 2 minutes. Melt remaining 2 tablespoons butter in 1-quart saucepan. Stir in flour. Cook 2 to 3 minutes, stirring constantly, until bubbly. Add milk; stir until thickened. Pour over chicken and mostaccioli in skillet. Heat 1 to 2 minutes.

Martha's Pizza Pie

Makes 6 servings
Preparation Time: 30 minutes; 20 minutes to bake

    2 quarts water
    2 teaspoons salt
  ½ pound extra-wide egg noodles
 1½ pounds bulk pork sausage
    2 tablespoons butter
  ½ cup chopped onion
    2 cloves garlic, minced
    1 8-ounce can tomato sauce
    1 6-ounce can tomato paste
    1 10-ounce package frozen mixed vegetables
  ¼ cup grated Parmesan cheese
 1½ teaspoons dried oregano
  ¼ teaspoon ground black pepper
    1 8-ounce can mushroom stems and pieces, drained
    1 green pepper, cored and sliced into rings
  ¼ cup pimiento-stuffed olives, sliced
    3 cups shredded mozzarella cheese, lightly packed

Preheat oven to 350°. Bring water to boil in deep pot. Add 1 teaspoon salt; stir in noodles. Cook, uncovered, 5 minutes, stirring occasionally. Drain; spread evenly over greased 12-inch pizza pan. Set aside. Brown sausage in large skillet over low heat, stirring to break up meat. Remove sausage; drain off grease. Wipe clean. Melt butter in skillet; saute onion and garlic until onion is translucent. Stir in tomato sauce, tomato paste, vegetables, Parmesan cheese, oregano, 1 teaspoon salt, and pepper. Bring to boil; remove from heat. Spoon over noodles in pan, spreading to edges. Top with mushrooms, green pepper and olives. Sprinkle with mozzarella cheese. Bake 20 minutes. Let stand 3 to 5 minutes before serving.

Chicken Napoli, this page
Cheese-Filled Meatballs, page 9

Homestyle

Homestyle Macaroni and Cheese

Makes 4 to 6 servings
Preparation Time: 20 minutes; 25 minutes to
bake

- ½ pound mostaccioli or macaroni
- ¼ cup butter
- ¼ cup flour
- 2¼ cups milk
- ¼ cup minced onion
- ½ teaspoon salt
- ½ teaspoon dry mustard
- 3 cups shredded Cheddar or process American cheese, lightly packed
  Sliced pimiento-stuffed olives, optional
  Tomato wedges to garnish, optional

Preheat oven to 350°. Grease 2½-quart casserole dish. Cook mostaccioli according to package directions; drain. Put in dish. Melt butter in 2-quart saucepan over medium heat. Add flour; cook, stirring until bubbly. Add milk, onion, salt and dry mustard. Stir until slightly thickened. Add cheese; stir until melted. Pour over mostaccioli. Bake 20 to 25 minutes. Let stand 5 minutes before serving. Garnish with pimento-stuffed olive slices and tomato wedges if desired.

Variation: Add 1 to 1½ cups diced cooked ham, chicken, turkey or luncheon meat to mostaccioli before topping with sauce. Reduce cheese to 2 cups.

Chicken Lasagne

Makes 8 to 10 servings
Preparation Time: 1 hour; 30 minutes to bake

- 1 cup chopped onion
- 2 cloves garlic, pressed
- ½ pound mushrooms, thinly sliced
- ½ cup butter
- 3 cups diced cooked chicken
- ¼ pound diced cooked ham
- 1 16-ounce can tomato puree
- ½ cup dry red wine
- 2 tablespoons minced parsley
- 1 teaspoon dried oregano
- 1 teaspoon dried basil
- 1 teaspoon salt
- ¼ teaspoon ground black pepper
- 10 ounces lasagne noodles
- 3 cups shredded mozzarella cheese, lightly packed
- ½ cup grated Parmesan cheese

Preheat oven to 350°. Grease 9 by 13-inch baking pan. Sauté onion, garlic and mushrooms in butter in 10-inch skillet over medium heat until onion is translucent. Stir in next 9 ingredients. Bring to a boil; cover. Cook 2 minutes. Cook lasagne according to package directions; drain well. Arrange ½ of noodles in pan. Spoon ½ of tomato mixture over noodles. Top with ½ of mozzarella cheese. Sprinkle with ½ of Parmesan cheese. Repeat layers. Bake 25 to 30 minutes.

Roman Rice Pie

Makes 4 to 6 servings
Preparation Time: 35 minutes; 25 minutes to
bake

- ½ cup uncooked rice
- 2 cups boiling water
- 1 teaspoon salt
- ½ cup chopped onion
- ½ cup chopped green pepper
- 2 tablespoons butter
- ½ teaspoon ground black pepper
- 2 cups shredded mozzarella cheese, lightly packed
- 3 tablespoons grated Parmesan cheese
- 1 egg, lightly beaten
- 1 pound lean ground beef
- 1 4-ounce can mushrooms, drained
- ¼ green pepper, cut in strips
- ½ small onion, cut in rings, separated
- ½ cup tomato sauce
- 2 tablespoons tomato paste
- 2 teaspoons dried oregano
- ¼ teaspoon garlic powder

Preheat oven to 400°. Grease 9-inch pie pan. Combine rice, boiling water and ½ teaspoon salt in large saucepan. Cover; cook 30 minutes. Sauté onion and green pepper in skillet in 1 tablespoon butter. Remove from heat; add ⅛ teaspoon pepper, ½ cup mozzarella cheese and 1 tablespoon Parmesan cheese. Stir in egg; mix well. Press firmly into pan to form crust. Brown beef with ½ teaspoon salt and ⅛ teaspoon pepper. Drain off fat; spoon meat into pan. Top with mushrooms, green pepper strips and onion rings. Mix tomato sauce, tomato paste, 1 tablespoon butter, 2 tablespoons Parmesan cheese, ¼ teaspoon pepper, oregano, and garlic powder; pour over pie. Bake 20 minutes. Sprinkle remaining 1½ cups mozzarella cheese on top; bake 5 minutes or until cheese melts. Let stand 3 minutes before serving.

Cheese-Filled Meatballs

Makes 6 servings
Preparation Time: 1 hour

1½ pounds ground beef chuck
2 tablespoons fine dry bread crumbs
2 eggs, lightly beaten
2 tablespoons grated onion
1 tablespoon minced parsley
1 teaspoon salt
½ teaspoon ground black pepper
4 ounces brick cheese, cut in ½-inch cubes
2 tablespoons vegetable oil
1 cup chopped onion
1 46-ounce can tomato juice
½ pound medium-size egg noodles

Mix beef, bread crumbs, eggs, grated onion, parsley, salt and ¼ teaspoon pepper in bowl. Shape around cheese cubes, making each meatball about 1½ inches in diameter. Heat oil in large kettle. Brown meatballs evenly on all sides. Remove; keep warm. Sauté onion in meat drippings until translucent. Add tomato juice and remaining ¼ teaspoon pepper. Heat to boiling. Stir in noodles gradually so that liquid continues to boil. Cook 5 minutes; add meatballs. Cover; simmer 7 minutes.

Chili con Carne

Makes 4 to 6 servings
Preparation Time: 15 minutes; 1½ hours to cook

1 pound ground beef chuck
1 large onion, chopped
½ cup chopped celery
⅓ cup chopped green pepper
1 16-ounce can whole tomatoes with liquid, chopped
1 6-ounce can tomato paste
2 cups hot water
2 to 3 tablespoons chili powder
1 tablespoon salt
2 teaspoons granulated sugar
1 teaspoon garlic powder
  Dash ground cinnamon
2 16-ounce cans Mexican-style chili beans or red kidney beans
  Chopped onion, optional
  Shredded Monterey Jack or Cheddar cheese, optional

Brown beef, onion, celery and green pepper in 3-quart saucepan, stirring to break up meat. Stir in next 8 ingredients; bring to boil. Add beans; cover; simmer 1½ hours, stirring occasionally. Serve topped with chopped onion and shredded cheese, if desired.

Cheese 'n Ham Strata

Makes 6 servings
Preparation Time: 15 minutes; 3 to 4 hours or overnight to chill; 30 minutes to bake

4½ cups cubed hard rolls or French bread
2 tablespoons butter, melted
2 cups cubed cooked ham
1½ cups grated Cheddar cheese, lightly packed
4 eggs
1½ cups milk
1 cup half-and-half
1 teaspoon instant minced onion
  Dash cayenne pepper

Grease 2½-quart baking dish. Spread bread cubes over bottom; drizzle with melted butter. Top with ham; sprinkle with cheese. Beat eggs in medium-size bowl. Stir in next 4 ingredients; pour over strata. Cover; chill 3 to 4 hours or overnight. Remove dish from refrigerator 30 minutes before baking. Preheat oven to 350°. Bake, uncovered, 30 minutes. Let stand 5 minutes before serving.

Broccoli Pasta

Makes 4 servings
Preparation Time: 15 minutes; 15 minutes to cook

½ pound lean ground beef
1 medium onion, chopped
2 cloves garlic, pressed
¼ cup butter
¼ cup chopped parsley
1 tablespoon lemon juice
1 tablespoon salt
1 teaspoon dried oregano
1 teaspoon dried basil or 1 tablespoon minced fresh basil
¼ teaspoon granulated sugar
¼ teaspoon ground black pepper
3 medium-size tomatoes, peeled and diced or 1 1-pound can Italian plum tomatoes, chopped
5 cups hot water
1 pound linguini or spaghetti
2 cups broccoli flowerets
1 cup crumbled feta cheese

Brown beef, onion and garlic in butter in large kettle, stirring to break up meat. Add next 9 ingredients. (If using canned tomatoes, add enough hot water to tomato juice to measure 5 cups.) Bring to boil; stir in next 3 ingredients. Return to boil. Cover; simmer 7 minutes. Remove from heat; let stand, covered, about 3 minutes.

Vegetarian Pizza

Makes 6 servings
Preparation Time: 20 minutes; 30 minutes for dough to rise; 30 minutes to bake

- 1 recipe Pizza Dough (see page 56)
- ½ pound mushrooms, sliced
- 1 clove garlic, pressed
- 2 tablespoons butter
- 1 8-ounce can tomato sauce
- 2 tablespoons grated Parmesan cheese
- 1½ teaspoons dried oregano
- ¼ teaspoon salt
- ⅛ teaspoon ground black pepper
- 1 cup sliced zucchini
- 1 14-ounce can whole artichokes, drained, quartered
- 1 cup onion rings
- ½ cup chopped green pepper
- 4 cups shredded mozzarella cheese, lightly packed

Grease 12 by 2-inch round pan. Press dough halfway up side of pan. Cover with kitchen towel; let rise until almost doubled in bulk, about 20 to 30 minutes. Preheat oven to 425°. Bake 20 minutes. Sauté mushrooms and garlic in butter. Add next 5 ingredients; bring to boil; cook 3 minutes. Uncover dough; spoon over sauce. Arrange next 4 ingredients over sauce; bake about 7 minutes. Sprinkle with cheese; bake 3 to 5 minutes. Let stand 2 to 3 minutes before serving.

Asparagus-Potato Scallop

Makes 5 to 6 servings
Preparation Time: 20 minutes; 40 minutes to bake

- 6 medium-size potatoes, peeled and cut into ¼-inch slices
- 1 15-ounce can whole asparagus spears, drained
- 1 10¾-ounce can condensed cream of celery soup
- 1 cup milk
- 2 cups shredded brick cheese, lightly packed
- ½ cup minced onion
- 3 tablespoons minced parsley
- ⅛ teaspoon ground white pepper
  Pimiento strips to garnish

Preheat oven to 350°. Grease 2-quart baking pan. Cook potato slices in small amount of boiling water in covered saucepan, about 8 minutes. Drain; arrange in pan. Top with asparagus spears. Mix next 6 ingredients; pour in pan. Bake 25 to 30 minutes. Let stand 5 to 10 minutes before serving. Garnish with pimiento strips.

Creamy Cheese Confetti

Makes 4 servings
Preparation Time: 25 minutes; 30 minutes to bake

- 2 cups elbow macaroni
- 2 tablespoons butter
- 2 tablespoons flour
- 1½ cups milk
- ½ teaspoon salt
- ¼ teaspoon hot pepper sauce
- 1½ cups shredded Cheddar cheese, lightly packed
- 2 cups chopped tomatoes
- 1 cup cooked broccoli flowerets

Preheat oven to 350°. Grease 2-quart casserole dish. Cook macaroni according to package directions; drain. Melt butter in 1-quart saucepan over medium heat. Add flour; cook, stirring until bubbly. Add milk; cook, stirring until thickened. Reduce heat to low; add salt, hot pepper sauce and cheese. Stir until cheese melts. Pour macaroni in dish. Mix in tomatoes and broccoli; top with cheese sauce. Bake 25 to 30 minutes.

Eggplant Parmigiana

Makes 6 servings
Preparation Time: 45 minutes; 45 minutes to cook

- 2 eggplants, quartered lengthwise
- 1½ teaspoons salt
- 3 cups sliced onion
- 3 large cloves garlic, minced
- ⅓ cup olive oil
- 1 16-ounce can tomatoes with juice, chopped
- 1 cup minced parsley
- ¼ cup water
- ¼ teaspoon ground black pepper
- 6 slices mozzarella cheese

Sprinkle eggplant slices with 1 teaspoon salt; let stand in colander 30 minutes. Sauté onion and garlic in olive oil in skillet until onion is translucent. Add next 4 ingredients and remaining ½ teaspoon salt. Rinse eggplant in lukewarm water; squeeze dry gently. Arrange eggplant in bottom of large kettle; top with onion mixture. Bring to boil; cover; simmer 45 minutes. Top with cheese slices; cover; heat about 2 minutes.

Note: Four sliced large tomatoes can be substituted for canned tomatoes.

Meatless

Spinach Squares

Makes 4 to 6 servings
Preparation Time: 20 minutes; 30 minutes to bake

- ¼ cup fine dry bread crumbs
- 1 7-ounce package elbow macaroni
- 1 10-ounce package frozen chopped spinach
- 4 eggs
- 1 cup ricotta cheese
- 1 cup grated Parmesan cheese
- ⅛ teaspoon ground white pepper
- 1 tablespoon butter, softened

Preheat oven to 350°. Grease 9-inch baking pan and sprinkle with bread crumbs. Cook macaroni according to package directions. Drain; set aside. Cook spinach according to package directions; drain well by pressing spinach against strainer using back of spoon. Beat 3 eggs, both cheeses and pepper in large bowl. Stir in macaroni and spinach; spoon into dish. Beat remaining egg; brush over spinach mixture, smoothing top. Bake 25 to 30 minutes. Brush top with butter.

Deviled Egg Casserole

Makes 4 servings
Preparation Time: 30 minutes; 10 minutes to bake

- 6 hard-cooked eggs, shelled and halved lengthwise
- ¼ cup mayonnaise
- ½ teaspoon salt
  Dash hot pepper sauce
- ¼ teaspoon paprika
- 1 teaspoon mustard
- 2 pounds asparagus, washed and trimmed or 1 10-ounce package frozen asparagus, cooked according to package directions
- 1 tablespoon butter
- 1 tablespoon flour
- ¼ teaspoon salt
- 1 cup milk
- ⅛ teaspoon hot pepper sauce
- 1 cup shredded Cheddar cheese, lightly packed

Preheat oven to 375°. Press egg yolks through sieve; mix with next 5 ingredients in bowl. Use to fill whites. Cook asparagus in small amount of salted boiling water in large covered skillet 5 to 10 minutes; drain. Put asparagus in 7 by 11-inch baking pan; top with egg halves. Melt butter in 1-quart saucepan over medium heat. Blend in flour and salt. Stir in milk gradually. Cook, stirring constantly, until mixture thickens and boils. Add hot pepper sauce and cheese, stirring until cheese melts. Pour over eggs. Bake 10 minutes.

Mediterranean Eggplant

Makes 6 servings
Preparation Time: 1½ hours; 40 minutes to cook; 1 hour to set

- 2 large eggplants, cut lengthwise in ¼-inch thick strips
- 1 tablespoon salt
- 4 medium-size onions, sliced lengthwise
- 3 cloves garlic, minced
- ½ cup olive oil
- 1 16-ounce can tomatoes with juice, chopped
- ½ cup minced parsley
- 1 teaspoon dried oregano
- ¼ teaspoon ground black pepper
- ½ cup uncooked rice
- 1 cup boiling water

Sprinkle both sides of eggplant strips with 2 teaspoons salt. Let stand in colander 30 to 60 minutes. Rinse with cold water; gently squeeze dry. Sauté onion and garlic in olive oil in skillet until onion is translucent. Add chopped tomatoes with juice, parsley, oregano, remaining 1 teaspoon salt and pepper. Bring to boil; set aside. Place ⅓ of eggplant in large kettle; top with ⅓ rice and ⅓ tomato sauce. Repeat layering with remaining eggplant, rice and tomato sauce. Pour boiling water around edge of kettle; bring to boil. Reduce heat; cover; simmer 40 minutes. Let stand 1 hour before serving.

Layered Casserole

Makes 6 servings
Preparation Time: 40 minutes; 30 minutes to bake

- 1 1½-pound eggplant
- 1 teaspoon salt
- ½ cup vegetable oil
- 1 pound zucchini, cut lengthwise into ⅛-inch slices
- 1 green pepper, cut into strips
- 1 egg
- ¼ cup milk
- ½ pound mostaccioli, cooked, drained
- 2 tablespoons grated Parmesan cheese
- 1 large tomato, thinly sliced
- 1 16-ounce carton cottage cheese with chives
- 1 cup shredded mozzarella cheese

Preheat oven to 350°. Grease 9 by 13-inch baking pan. Coat a large baking sheet with oil; set aside. Peel eggplant partially, leaving some skin. Cut crosswise in ⅛-inch slices; sprinkle with salt. Drain in colander 20 minutes. Rinse off salt; lightly squeeze slices to remove excess water. Place on baking sheet; brush with ¼ cup oil. Broil 10 minutes on each side until golden brown. Remove eggplant slices; place zucchini on baking sheet. Brush with remaining ¼ cup oil; broil 10 minutes on each side until golden brown. Remove zucchini slices; pour excess oil in small skillet. Sauté green pepper until golden. Beat egg and milk in bowl; pour over mostaccioli; sprinkle with Parmesan cheese; toss again. Layer in this order in dish: mostaccioli mixture, zucchini, green pepper, tomato slices, eggplant and cottage cheese with chives. Sprinkle with shredded mozzarella cheese; bake 30 minutes. Let stand 5 minutes before serving.

Herb Cheese Casserole

Makes 6 to 8 servings
Preparation Time: 15 minutes; 1 hour to bake

    3 cups elbow macaroni
    1 cup chopped onion
    1 cup chopped celery
    1 clove garlic, pressed
    ¼ cup butter
    ¼ cup chopped pimiento
    ¼ cup chopped parsley
    6 eggs
    2 cups milk
    2 teaspoons salt
    ⅛ teaspoon ground black pepper
    1 teaspoon dried oregano
    1 teaspoon Worcestershire sauce
    2 16-ounce cartons creamed cottage cheese
    ¼ cup grated Parmesan cheese
    1 medium-size tomato, sliced
    1 tablespoon grated Parmesan cheese

Preheat oven to 350°. Grease shallow 3-quart casserole or 9 by 13-inch baking pan. Cook macaroni according to package directions; drain. Sauté onion, celery and garlic in butter in skillet until onion is translucent; stir in pimiento and parsley. Beat eggs with next 5 ingredients in bowl. Stir in cottage cheese, ¼ cup Parmesan cheese, onion mixture and cooked macaroni; pour in dish. Cover; bake 1 hour. Arrange tomato slices over casserole; sprinkle with 1 tablespoon Parmesan cheese; bake, uncovered, 15 minutes.

Tabbouleh Salad

Makes 4 servings
Preparation Time: 30 minutes; 1 hour to chill

    2 cups bulgur or cracked wheat
    4 cups hot water
    2 cups minced parsley
    1 cup minced celery
    1 cup minced onion
    2 cups seeded, diced tomatoes
    ¾ cup olive or vegetable oil
    ¾ cup fresh lemon juice
    2 teaspoons salt
    ½ teaspoon ground black pepper
    ¼ teaspoon garlic powder
       Thin lemon slices, twisted

Pour hot water over bulgur in bowl; let stand 30 minutes. Drain; put in large bowl. Add next 4 ingredients. Beat next 5 ingredients in bowl with fork; pour over bulgur. Toss well. Cover; chill 1 to 2 hours. Garnish with lemon twists.

Spinach Strudel

Makes 4 servings
Preparation Time: 40 minutes; 35 minutes to bake

   10 ounces spinach, washed, thinly sliced
    1 tablespoon salt
    1 17¼-ounce package frozen puff pastry
    1 leek, washed, drained and thinly sliced
    2 cups thinly sliced mushrooms
    ¼ cup butter
    1 cup ricotta cheese
    1 8-ounce package cream cheese
    ¼ cup grated Parmesan cheese
    2 eggs, lightly beaten
    ¼ cup finely crushed salted crackers
    ¼ teaspoon dried thyme
    ¼ teaspoon dried oregano
    1 egg, lightly beaten

Put spinach in colander; sprinkle with salt; let stand 30 minutes. Squeeze well to remove excess water. Thaw pastry at room temperature 20 minutes. Sauté spinach, leek and mushrooms in butter in skillet. Remove from heat; cool slightly. Stir in next 7 ingredients. Unfold pastry sheets; cut each in 4 pieces. Roll each piece on lightly floured surface to 7-inch square. Place about ¼ cup filling down center of each square. Fold one side of dough over to cover filling. Fold remaining dough over. Repeat with remaining squares. Pinch edges. Place folded-side-down on baking sheet. Brush tops with egg. Bake in 350° preheated oven 35 minutes.

Parmesan Chicken

Makes 4 servings
Preparation Time: 20 minutes; 1 hour to bake

    1   cup grated Parmesan cheese
    1   3-ounce can French-fried onions, crushed
    ¼   cup dry bread crumbs
    ½   teaspoon paprika
    ½   teaspoon salt
    ¼   teaspoon onion powder
        Dash cayenne pepper
    1   egg
    2   tablespoons milk
    1   3-pound broiler-fryer chicken, cut in serving pieces
    4   small zucchini, halved lengthwise
    2   tablespoons butter, softened
    4   crab apples

Preheat oven to 375°. Combine ¾ cup Parmesan cheese and next 6 ingredients in shallow pan. Beat egg and milk in another shallow pan. Dip chicken pieces in egg-milk mixture; then in cheese mixture. Arrange skin-side-up in 10 by 15-inch jelly roll pan. (Pieces should not touch.) Bake 45 minutes. Remove from oven. Arrange zucchini halves around chicken; brush with butter; sprinkle with remaining ¼ cup Parmesan cheese. Bake 15 minutes. Garnish with crab apples.

Beef Brisket

Makes 8 to 10 servings
Preparation Time: 15 minutes; 3½ hours to bake

    3   to 3½ pounds boneless beef brisket
    2   10½-ounce cans condensed beef consommé
    ¼   cup dry red wine
    2   cloves garlic, pressed
    ¼   teaspoon dried basil
    ¼   teaspoon ground black pepper
    1   bay leaf
    1   cup thinly sliced onion
    1   pound mushrooms, thinly sliced
    8   small potatoes, halved
    8   small carrots, halved

Preheat oven to 325°. Put brisket in large 2-inch deep baking pan. Mix next 6 ingredients in 1-quart saucepan; bring to boil. Pour over meat; top with sliced onion. Cover; bake 2½ hours. Add next 3 ingredients; cover; bake about 1 hour. Serve meat with vegetables and pan juices.

Taco Casserole

Makes 6 servings
Preparation Time: 20 minutes; 25 minutes to bake

    1½ pounds lean ground beef
    1   10-ounce can mild enchilada sauce
    2   15-ounce cans black-eyed peas, drained
    1   15-ounce can tomatoes with juice, cut up
    1   teaspoon granulated sugar
    ½   teaspoon salt
    ⅛   teaspoon ground black pepper
    3   cups shredded Cheddar cheese, lightly packed
    1   head lettuce, shredded
    1   green pepper, cored and chopped
    1   medium-size onion, chopped
        Corn chips, to garnish

Preheat oven to 350°. Brown beef in 10-inch skillet, stirring to break up meat. Drain off fat; stir in next 6 ingredients; simmer 10 minutes. Layer ½ mixture in 3-quart round casserole; sprinkle with ½ of cheese. Mix lettuce, green pepper and onion; arrange over cheese. Top with remaining meat; sprinkle with remaining cheese. Bake 20 to 25 minutes. Garnish with warm corn chips.

Note: To warm corn chips, place in 300° degree oven on a baking sheet until crispy, about 5 minutes.

Ham with Yams

Makes 4 servings
Preparation Time: 20 minutes

    1   pound fully cooked ½-inch thick ham slice
    1   tablespoon butter
    1   1-pound 4-ounce can sliced pineapple
    1   tablespoon cornstarch
    1   1-pound 8-ounce can yams in syrup
    ⅓   cup light brown sugar, firmly packed
        Dash ground cloves

Brown ham on both sides in butter in large skillet over medium heat, about 4 to 5 minutes per side; set aside. Drain pineapple slices reserving ½ cup juice and 4 slices. Dissolve cornstarch in pineapple juice; pour in 1-quart saucepan. Drain yams; reserving ½ cup syrup. Add syrup to pineapple juice mixture; stir in brown sugar and cloves. Cook, stirring until slightly thickened. Arrange yams around ham. Top with pineapple slices. Top with pineapple sauce; heat through before serving.

Meat

Moussaka

Makes 4 to 6 servings
Preparation Time: 45 minutes; 1 hour to bake

- 1 **pound eggplant, cut in ¼-inch thick lengthwise strips**
- 2 **teaspoons salt**
- 1 **pound lean ground beef**
- 1 **medium-size onion, chopped**
- 1 **clove garlic, minced**
- 1 **8-ounce can tomato sauce**
- 1 **cup diagonally sliced celery**
- 1 **teaspoon dried oregano**
- ¼ **teaspoon ground black pepper**
- 4 **medium-size potatoes, pared, cut in ¼-inch thick crosswise slices**
- 1 **pound zucchini, cut in ¼-inch thick lengthwise strips**

Sprinkle eggplant slices with 1 teaspoon salt. Place in colander; let stand 30 minutes. Brown beef, onion and garlic in 10-inch skillet, stirring to break up meat. Add tomato sauce, celery, oregano, remaining 1 teaspoon salt and pepper; bring to boil; remove from heat. Preheat oven to 350°. Rinse eggplant slices in lukewarm water; squeeze gently. Spread about ¼ cup sauce in 9 by 13-inch baking pan. Arrange potatoes in bottom; top with ⅓ of sauce. Top with eggplant slices. Cover with ⅓ of sauce. Top with zucchini slices. Spoon remaining sauce over top; cover. Bake 50 to 60 minutes.

Lamb Celery Espagnole

Makes 4 servings
Preparation Time: 10 minutes; 1 hour 20 minutes to cook

- 2 **pounds lamb shoulder, cut in 3-inch pieces**
- 1 **tablespoon lemon juice**
- 1 **cup chopped onion**
- 1 **clove garlic, minced**
- 1 **tablespoon butter**
- 1½ **teaspoons salt**
- ¼ **teaspoon ground black pepper**
- 1½ **cups hot water**
- 1 **6-ounce can tomato paste**
- 8 **cups diagonally sliced 1-inch celery pieces with leaves**
  Lemon wedges, optional

Sprinkle lamb with lemon juice. Brown lamb, onion and garlic in butter in large kettle over medium-high heat. Sprinkle with salt and pepper. Add water and tomato paste; bring to boil. Reduce heat; cover. Simmer 45 minutes. Add celery; bring to boil. Cover; simmer 35 minutes. Squeeze fresh lemon juice over each portion before serving, if desired.

Bavarian Supper

Makes 4 servings
Preparation Time: 15 minutes; 30 minutes to bake

- 8 **frankfurters _or_ 8 precooked bratwurst**
- 2 **medium-size onions, chopped**
- 1 **1-pound 13-ounce can sauerkraut, drained**
- 2 **medium-size potatoes, pared, halved and thinly sliced**
- 2 **tablespoons butter**
- 1 **12-ounce can beer**
- 1 **8-ounce can tomato sauce**
- 1 **tablespoon brown sugar, firmly packed**
- 1 **teaspoon caraway seed**
- ¼ **teaspoon salt**
  Dash hot pepper sauce

Preheat oven to 375°. Make 3 crosswise slits in each frankfurter. Sauté onions, sauerkraut and potatoes in butter in skillet 5 minutes. Stir in next 6 ingredients; heat to boiling. Pour in 7 by 11-inch baking pan. Top with frankfurters; bake 30 minutes.

Stuffed Cabbage

Makes 4 servings
Preparation Time: 30 minutes; 1 hour to bake

- 1 **medium-size cabbage, about 1½ pounds, quartered vertically**
- 1½ **pounds ground beef chuck**
- ½ **cup chopped onion**
- 1 **clove garlic, minced**
- 1¼ **teaspoons salt**
- 1 **teaspoon dried oregano**
- ¼ **teaspoon ground black pepper**
- 2 **medium-size potatoes, pared, quartered lengthwise, thinly sliced**
- ½ **cup shredded carrots**
- ½ **cup bread crumbs**
- ⅓ **cup chopped parsley**
- 1 **8-ounce can tomato sauce**
- 1 **cup shredded Cheddar cheese, lightly packed**
- 1 **teaspoon butter**
- ¾ **cup water**
- 1 **tablespoon butter**

Preheat oven to 350°. Scoop out some cabbage from center of each quarter to equal 4 cups; set aside. Brown meat, onion, garlic, 1 teaspoon salt, oregano and pepper in skillet, stirring to break up meat. Remove from heat. Stir in potatoes, carrots, bread crumbs, parsley, ¾ cup tomato sauce and cheese. Spoon into cabbage quarters; dot each with butter. Place in 9 by 13-inch baking pan. Blend remaining ¼ cup tomato sauce, water, 1 tablespoon butter and remaining ¼ teaspoon salt; pour into pan. Cover tightly; bake 55 to 60 minutes.

Note: Leftover 4 cups of cabbage can be used to make coleslaw, if desired.

Stuffed Green Peppers

Makes 4 servings
Preparation Time: 30 minutes; 1 hour to bake

    1 pound ground beef
    ½ cup chopped onion
    1 clove garlic, pressed
    1 teaspoon salt
    ¼ teaspoon ground black pepper
    1 15-ounce can tomato sauce
    ½ cup uncooked rice
    ½ cup minced parsley
    1 teaspoon dried dill weed
    6 large green peppers, cut in half lengthwise, seeded
    ½ cup hot water
    1 tablespoon butter
   12 thin slices tomato
      Grated Parmesan cheese

Preheat oven to 450°. Brown first 5 ingredients in 10-inch skillet, stirring to break up meat. Add ¾ of tomato sauce and next 3 ingredients; bring to boil; remove from heat. Fill peppers with mixture; place in 9 by 13-inch baking pan. Mix remaining tomato sauce with hot water and butter in bowl. Pour around peppers in pan. Top each pepper with 1 tomato slice. Sprinkle with Parmesan cheese. Cover; bake 15 minutes. Reduce oven temperature to 350°; bake 30 minutes. Uncover; bake 10 to 15 minutes.

Shepherd's Beef Pie

Makes 4 servings
Preparation Time: 25 minutes; 1¾ hours to bake

    2 tablespoons flour
    1 teaspoon salt
    ⅛ teaspoon ground black pepper
   1½ pounds boneless beef chuck, cut in 1½-inch cubes
      Flour
    1 tablespoon vegetable oil
    1 tablespoon butter
    1 cup chopped onion
    1 cup beef broth
    1 tablespoon Worcestershire sauce
    ½ teaspoon margarine
    ¼ teaspoon dried thyme
    1 cup 1-inch carrot slices
    1 cup 1-inch celery pieces
    1 10-ounce package frozen peas, thawed
    2 cups hot mashed potatoes
    2 tablespoons butter, melted
      Paprika

Preheat oven to 350°. Mix flour, ½ teaspoon salt and pepper. Dredge beef in flour. Heat oil and butter in large kettle with cover. Brown beef on medium-high heat evenly on all sides. Add onion; cook until translucent. Add next 4 ingredients. Cover; bake 1 hour. Add carrot and celery; sprinkle with remaining ½ teaspoon salt. Cover; bake 30 minutes. Fold in peas; transfer to 1½-quart round casserole dish. Drop large spoonfuls of potato around edge of dish; brush with butter; sprinkle with paprika. Increase oven temperature to 400°. Bake 15 minutes.

Salisbury Steak Dinner

Makes 4 to 6 servings
Preparation Time: 20 minutes; 1 hour to bake

   1½ pounds lean ground beef
    1 10½-ounce can condensed onion soup
    ½ cup fine dry bread crumbs
    2 eggs, lightly beaten
    2 tablespoons catsup
    2 tablespoons grated Parmesan cheese
    ½ teaspoon onion salt
    ⅛ teaspoon ground black pepper
    1 tablespoon vegetable oil
    ¼ cup flour
    ¼ cup beef broth
    ¼ cup catsup
    1 teaspoon Worcestershire sauce
    1 teaspoon granulated sugar
    ½ teaspoon dry mustard
    2 cups hot mashed potatoes
    2 tablespoons butter, melted
      Paprika

Preheat oven to 350°. Combine beef, ¼ cup onion soup, bread crumbs, eggs, 2 tablespoons catsup, 1 tablespoon Parmesan cheese, onion salt and pepper. Shape into 6 oval patties. Brush large skillet with oil. Dip patties lightly in flour; brown on both sides over medium heat. Pour off fat. Arrange in 9 by 13-inch baking pan. Mix remaining onion soup, beef broth, ¼ cup catsup, Worcestershire sauce, sugar and dry mustard in small bowl. Pour into skillet; heat, stirring to loosen browned bits. Pour over patties; cover with foil; bake 25 minutes. Turn patties; cover; bake 20 minutes. Remove cover; drop large spoonfuls of mashed potatoes around edges; brush with butter; sprinkle with remaining 1 tablespoon Parmesan cheese and paprika. Bake 20 minutes.

Meat

New England Boiled Dinner

Makes 8 to 10 servings
Preparation Time: 30 minutes; 2 hours 15 minutes to cook

2½ to 3 pound boneless corned beef brisket
  2 cloves garlic, halved
  1 tablespoon mixed whole pickling spice
  9 small onions
  6 medium-size carrots, halved
  4 medium-size potatoes, halved
  2 turnips, pared and cubed
  1 small cabbage, cut in 8 wedges

Put enough cold water in large kettle to just cover beef. Tie garlic and spice in cheesecloth bag; add to kettle. Quarter 1 onion; add to kettle. Bring to boil; reduce heat. Cover; simmer about 1½ hours. Add remaining whole onions, carrots, potatoes and turnips. Bring to boil. Cover; simmer 30 minutes. Add cabbage; bring to boil. Simmer, uncovered, 15 minutes.

Note: To carve meat, place fat-side-up on platter or cutting board. Carve across grain in thin slices starting at pointed end.

Biscuit Beef Pie

Makes 4 to 5 servings
Preparation Time: 2 hours; 15 minutes to bake

  1 pound beef stew meat
1¼ cups flour
  2 tablespoons vegetable oil
2½ cups water
  1 small bay leaf
  1 cup sliced green beans, *or* frozen sliced green beans, thawed
  2 small onions, thinly sliced
  4 small carrots, thinly sliced
  4 small potatoes, cut in 1-inch cubes
  ½ cup diced green pepper
1¾ teaspoons salt
  ⅛ teaspoon ground black pepper
  1 tablespoon water
  1 teaspoon baking powder
  3 tablespoons shortening
  ⅓ cup milk

Roll meat in 3 tablespoons flour; brown on all sides in hot oil in 10-inch skillet. Add water and bay leaf; cover; bring to boil. Reduce heat; simmer 1 hour. Add beans, onions, carrots, potatoes, green pepper, 1½ teaspoons salt and pepper; simmer 30 minutes. Blend 1 tablespoon flour and 1 tablespoon water together; stir into meat mixture; bring to a boil. Spoon into 8-inch square baking pan. Preheat oven to 450°. Sift together remaining 1 cup flour, baking powder and remaining ¼ teaspoon salt. Cut in shortening. Add milk, mixing only until blended. Roll into 6-inch square on floured surface. Cut into 4 pieces. Place biscuit squares on top of meat in pan; bake 15 minutes.

German-Style Salad with Frankfurters

Makes 4 servings
Preparation Time: 1 hour

  8 slices bacon, chopped
  4 green onions, sliced
  1 tablespoon flour
  ¾ cup water
  ⅓ cup white vinegar
  2 teaspoons mustard
  2 tablespoons granulated sugar
  1 teaspoon salt
  ¼ teaspoon ground black pepper
  6 frankfurters *or* 4 knockwurst *or* ½ pound ring bologna, cut diagonally in ½-inch pieces
  4 medium-size potatoes, cooked, peeled, halved lengthwise and cut in ⅛-inch slices
  ¼ cup minced parsley

Cook bacon in large skillet until brown. Add onions and flour; cook until bubbly. Add next 6 ingredients; bring to boil. Add franks; bring to boil. Cook 3 minutes over medium heat. Stir in potatoes and parsley gently, coating potatoes with sauce. Bring to boil; remove from heat; serve immediately.

Potato Pork Casserole

Makes 4 servings
Preparation Time: 10 minutes; 1 hour 15 minutes to bake

  4 ½-inch thick rib *or* loin pork chops
  1 10½-ounce can condensed cream of mushroom soup
  1 medium-size onion, chopped
  1 teaspoon salt
  ¼ teaspoon ground black pepper
  ½ teaspoon dried oregano
  1 tablespoon chopped parsley
  3 cups thinly sliced potatoes
    Paprika

Preheat oven to 350°. Brown chops on both sides in 10-inch skillet. Pour off drippings. Mix next 6 ingredients; pour half in 9 by 13-inch baking pan. Arrange potatoes in pan; top with chops. Top with remaining soup mixture; sprinkle with paprika. Cover; bake 1 hour. Uncover; bake 15 minutes.

New England Boiled Dinner, this page

Meat

Oven-Barbecued Drumsticks

Makes 4 servings
Preparation Time: 15 minutes; 2 hours to bake

- 2 turkey drumsticks, about 3 pounds
- 1 teaspoon salt
- ¼ teaspoon ground black pepper
- 2 tablespoons vegetable oil
- 3 tablespoons unsulphured molasses
- 1½ tablespoons mustard
- 2 tablespoons white wine vinegar
- 1 teaspoon Worcestershire sauce
- ⅛ teaspoon hot pepper sauce
- ⅛ teaspoon garlic powder
- 2 carrots, cut in 1½-inch pieces
- 4 medium-size baking potatoes, halved
- ¼ cup shredded Cheddar cheese

Preheat oven to 375°. Rub drumsticks with salt and pepper. Blend next 7 ingredients in bowl. Roll drumsticks in barbecue mixture. Place on large sheet of foil in large shallow baking pan. Pour remaining mixture over drumsticks; cover loosely with foil. Bake 1 hour. Open foil package; arrange carrots and potatoes around drumsticks. Brush potato tops with barbecue mixture in foil. Bake 1 hour, brushing drumsticks and potatoes occasionally with barbecue mixture. Sprinkle with cheese 5 minutes before potatoes are done.

Garbanzo Lamb Stew

Makes 4 servings
Preparation Time: 1½ hours

- 2 pounds lamb shoulder, cut in 3-inch pieces
- 1 tablespoon lemon juice
- 1 cup chopped onion
- ¼ cup chopped celery
- ¼ cup chopped carrot
- 1 clove garlic, pressed
- 1 tablespoon butter
- 1 teaspoon salt
- ⅛ teaspoon ground black pepper
- 1 cup hot water
- 1 16-ounce can sliced stewed tomatoes with juice
- 1 bay leaf
- 2 15-ounce cans garbanzo beans, drained

Sprinkle lamb with lemon juice. Brown with onion, celery, carrot and garlic in butter in large skillet. Sprinkle with salt and pepper. Add water, tomatoes with juice and bay leaf; bring to boil. Cover; simmer 45 minutes. Add garbanzo beans; bring to boil. Cover; simmer 15 minutes.

Creole Beef Stew

Makes 6 servings
Preparation Time: 15 minutes; 2½ hours to cook

- 3 tablespoons vegetable oil
- 1½ pounds beef stew meat, trimmed of excess fat and cut in 1-inch cubes
- 1 tablespoon flour
- 2 teaspoons salt
- ¼ teaspoon ground black pepper
- 2 medium-size onions, sliced
- ½ cup chopped green pepper
- 1 clove garlic, pressed
- 3 cups hot water
- 1 14½-ounce can stewed tomatoes with juice, sliced
- 1 bay leaf
- 1 teaspoon chili powder
- 3 medium-size potatoes
- 1 16-ounce package frozen okra
- 1 tablespoon lemon juice

Heat oil in large kettle over medium heat. Add meat; sprinkle with flour, 1 teaspoon salt and pepper. Brown evenly on all sides. Add onion, green pepper, and garlic during last few minutes of browning. Add 2 cups hot water, tomatoes with juice and bay leaf; bring to boil. Cover; simmer 1½ hours. Remove bay leaf; add remaining 1 cup water, remaining 1 teaspoon salt, chili powder and potatoes. Bring to boil; cover; simmer 15 minutes. Add okra and lemon juice; bring to boil. Cover; simmer 10 to 12 minutes.

Pot Roast in Foil

Makes 4 to 6 servings
Preparation Time: 15 minutes; 3 hours to bake

- 2 to 3 pounds boneless *or* bone-in beef chuck blade pot roast
- 1 1½-ounce package spaghetti sauce mix
- 1 teaspoon salt
- ⅛ teaspoon ground black pepper
- 4 medium-size carrots, halved crosswise
- 4 medium-size potatoes, halved
- 4 stalks celery, cut in 2-inch pieces
- 4 small onions, cut in rings
- 10 small pimiento-stuffed olives

Preheat oven to 350°. Put roast on piece of heavy-duty foil on jelly roll pan. Combine spaghetti sauce mix, salt and pepper. Rub on both sides of roast. Arrange carrots, potatoes and celery around roast. Top with onion rings and olives. Fold foil over; seal tightly. Bake 2½ to 3 hours.

Bacon Bean Bake

Makes 6 servings
Preparation Time: 10 minutes; 30 minutes to bake

- 1 pound bacon, cooked, drained and coarsely crumbled
- 1 cup chopped onion
- 1 cup diagonally sliced celery
- 2 15-ounce cans lima beans, drained
- 2 15-ounce cans kidney beans, drained
- ½ cup light corn syrup
- ½ cup mild enchilada sauce
- 1 teaspoon chili powder
- 1 teaspoon salt
- ¼ teaspoon garlic powder

Preheat oven to 350°. Mix all ingredients in 3-quart baking pan. Cover; bake 30 minutes.

Old World Casserole

Makes 4 servings
Preparation Time: 30 minutes; 1 hour to bake

- 2 tablespoons butter, softened
- 1½ pounds ground chuck
- ⅓ cup fine dry bread crumbs
- ¾ cup evaporated milk
- 1 small onion, grated
- 2 teaspoons salt
- ¼ teaspoon ground black pepper
- ½ teaspoon mint leaves, crushed
- ⅛ teaspoon garlic powder
- 4 medium-size potatoes, peeled and sliced
- 1 small onion, chopped
- 1 cup tomato juice

Preheat oven to 375°. Coat 9 by 13-inch baking pan with butter. Mix ground chuck, bread crumbs, milk, grated onion, 1½ teaspoons salt, pepper, mint leaves and garlic powder in bowl. Shape into 8 round patties. Arrange potatoes and chopped onion in baking pan; sprinkle with remaining ½ teaspoon salt. Top with beef patties. Pour tomato juice over all. Bake 30 minutes; turn patties; bake 30 minutes.

Pork Chops Orient

Makes 4 servings
Preparation Time: 45 minutes

- 1½ tablespoons flour
- ¼ teaspoon salt
- ⅛ teaspoon ground black pepper
- 6 ½-inch thick loin *or* rib pork chops
- 1 tablespoon vegetable oil
- ¼ cup soy sauce
- 1 16-ounce package frozen oriental-style vegetables, thawed
- ¼ teaspoon garlic powder

Mix flour, salt and pepper. Dredge chops in flour. Brown in oil in 12-inch skillet over medium heat, about 7 minutes per side. Cover; simmer 20 to 25 minutes. Remove; keep warm. Increase heat to medium-high; add soy sauce to drippings in skillet. Add vegetables; sprinkle with garlic powder. Cook, stirring, until vegetables are tender, but crisp, about 4 to 5 minutes. Add chops; heat through.

Meat Loaf Succotash

Makes 4 servings
Preparation Time: 15 minutes; 1 hour 15 minutes to bake

- 1 pound lean ground beef
- ½ cup minced onion
- ½ cup beef broth
- 2 tablespoons dry bread crumbs
- ½ teaspoon salt
- ½ teaspoon garlic powder
- ½ teaspoon cumin
- ⅛ teaspoon ground black pepper
  Flour
- ½ cup tomato sauce
- 2 10-ounce packages frozen succotash, thawed

Preheat oven to 350°. Mix beef, onion, ¼ cup broth, bread crumbs, salt, garlic powder, cumin and pepper in bowl. Shape into loaf; roll lightly in flour. Place in 7 by 11-inch baking pan. Mix tomato sauce with remaining ¼ cup broth; pour over meat loaf. Bake 1 hour. Arrange succotash around meat loaf. Bake 15 minutes.

Pork Steaks Rio Grande

Makes 6 servings
Preparation Time: 15 minutes; 50 minutes to bake

- 6 ½-inch thick pork steaks
- 1 teaspoon salt
- ¾ cup uncooked rice
- 1½ cups hot water
- 1 8-ounce can tomato sauce
- ½ package taco seasoning mix, about 1½ tablespoons
- 6 ½-inch green pepper rings
- ½ cup shredded Cheddar cheese, lightly packed

Preheat oven to 350°. Brown chops in large skillet over medium heat. Drain off fat; arrange in 9 by 13-inch baking pan. Sprinkle with salt; arrange rice around chops. Combine water, tomato sauce and seasoning mix in bowl; pour over chops and rice. Cover tightly with foil; bake 40 minutes. Arrange pepper slices over chops; sprinkle cheese in center of pepper rings. Cover; bake 10 minutes.

Eggs & Cheese

Deluxe Denver Combo

Makes 2 servings
Preparation Time: 15 minutes

- 2 tablespoons butter
- 1 cup diced cooked ham
- 1 cup frozen hash brown potatoes, thawed
- 2 tablespoons chopped green pepper
- 2 tablespoons sliced green onion
- ¼ cup sliced mushrooms
- 4 eggs
- ¼ teaspoon salt
  Dash hot pepper sauce
- 2 tablespoons dairy sour cream or plain yogurt
- 1 small tomato, peeled, seeded, chopped and drained

Melt butter in 10-inch skillet. Add next 5 ingredients; cook, stirring until potatoes are tender. Beat eggs, salt and hot pepper sauce in bowl. Pour over ham mixture; cook until eggs are set, carefully lifting edges with metal spatula so uncooked portion can flow underneath. Cut in half; slide one-half omelet onto warm plate. Top with ½ tablespoon sour cream and ½ chopped tomato. Repeat with remaining half of omelet, sour cream and chopped tomato.

Berry Yogurt Omelet

Makes 2 servings
Preparation Time: 15 minutes

- 4 eggs
- ¼ cup milk
- ⅛ teaspoon salt
- 1 tablespoon butter
- ½ cup strawberry or raspberry yogurt
- 1¼ cups sliced strawberries or whole raspberries

Beat eggs, milk and salt. Heat butter in 10-inch omelet pan until drop of water sizzles when added to pan. Add eggs. Slide metal spatula around edge of pan, lifting eggs so uncooked portion will flow underneath. Spread 2 tablespoons strawberry yogurt over half of omelet. Sprinkle with ¼ cup yogurt; fold omelet in half or roll. Transfer to platter; top with remaining yogurt. Top with strawberries. Serve immediately.

Zucchini Bake

Makes 4 servings
Preparation Time: 15 minutes; 50 minutes to bake

- 2 tablespoons butter
- ¾ cup finely crushed cornflake crumbs
- 3 cups shredded zucchini
- ½ cup minced onion
- ½ cup minced celery
- ½ cup grated Parmesan cheese
- ¼ cup shredded carrot
- 2 tablespoons minced parsley
- ¾ teaspoon salt
- 1 teaspoon dried oregano
- ½ teaspoon dried dillweed
- 6 eggs
- ½ cup half-and-half

Preheat oven to 350°. Grease 9-inch square baking pan with butter. Sprinkle with half of cornflake crumbs. Mix next 9 ingredients in large bowl. Beat eggs and half-and-half in bowl. Pour over zucchini mixture; blend; pour into pan. Sprinkle with remaining cornflake crumbs. Bake 50 minutes; let stand 10 minutes before serving.

Potato Omelet

Makes 2 servings
Preparation Time: 20 minutes

- 2 tablespoons butter
- 2 medium-size potatoes, pared and thinly sliced
- ½ cup sliced onion
- 1 tablespoon minced parsley
- ⅛ teaspoon paprika
- 4 eggs
- ¼ cup milk
- ½ teaspoon salt
  Freshly ground black pepper
- 1 small tomato, chopped

Melt butter in 10-inch skillet. Add next 4 ingredients; cover; cook 5 minutes over low heat, stirring twice. Uncover; cook 3 to 5 minutes until potatoes are golden brown and tender. Beat eggs, milk, salt and pepper in bowl. Pour over potatoes; cook until eggs are almost set, about 3 minutes. Slide onto serving plate; spoon tomato on top. Serve immediately.

Deluxe Denver Combo, this page

Eggs & Cheese

Eggs Bechamel

Makes 6 servings
Preparation Time: 30 minutes; 20 minutes to bake

- ¼ cup butter
- ¼ cup flour
- 1½ cups milk
- ½ teaspoon salt
  Dash ground nutmeg
- 6 hard-cooked eggs, shelled and halved lengthwise
- 2 tablespoons minced green onion
- 1 pound broccoli, cooked, drained and cut into spears, *or* 2 10-ounce packages frozen broccoli spears, cooked and drained
- 1 cup shredded Swiss cheese, lightly packed
  Paprika

Preheat oven to 350°. Melt butter in 2-quart saucepan. Stir in flour; cook until bubbly. Add milk; cook, stirring over medium heat until mixture thickens. Remove from heat; stir in salt and nutmeg. Remove egg yolks from whites; mash with fork. Add 2 tablespoons sauce and green onion; blend well. Fill egg halves with yolk mixture. Arrange broccoli spears in 7 by 11-inch baking pan; surround with egg halves. Top with sauce; sprinkle with cheese. Bake 15 to 20 minutes. Sprinkle with paprika.

Eggs Rancheros

Makes 2 to 3 servings
Preparation Time: 20 minutes

- ½ pound ground beef
- ⅛ teaspoon garlic powder
- 3 tablespoons butter
- ½ cup chopped onion
- ½ cup chopped celery
- ½ cup chopped green pepper
- 2 teaspoons chili powder
- ¾ teaspoon salt
- 1 cup chopped, seeded tomatoes with juice
- 1 cup shredded Cheddar cheese, lightly packed
- 4 eggs
- 2 tablespoons milk
- ½ cup dairy sour cream *or* unflavored yogurt
- 2 tablespoons minced parsley

Brown beef with garlic powder in 10-inch skillet, stirring to break up meat. Drain off fat; add 1 tablespoon butter, next 4 ingredients and ½ teaspoon salt. Cook; stirring until onion is translucent. Stir in tomatoes; simmer until heated through. Stir in cheese until melted. Beat eggs, milk and ¼ teaspoon salt in small bowl. Melt remaining 2 tablespoons butter in 9-inch omelet pan or skillet over medium heat. Pour in eggs; cook until light brown on bottom. Slide metal spatula around edge of skillet, lifting egg mixture to let uncooked portion flow underneath. Cook 15 to 20 seconds; fold omelet in half in pan; slide onto warm plate. Top with sauce and sour cream; sprinkle with parsley.

Autumn Apple Scramble

Makes 2 servings
Preparation Time: 15 minutes

- 1 small potato, thinly sliced
- ⅛ teaspoon salt
- 3 tablespoons butter
- 1 red cooking apple, thinly sliced
- ½ cup diced cooked ham
- 2 teaspoons brown sugar, firmly packed
- 3 eggs
- 1 tablespoon milk *or* cream

Sprinkle potato with salt. Cook in 1 tablespoon butter in skillet over medium heat 4 minutes. Add apple and ham; sprinkle with brown sugar. Mix; cover; cook 2 to 3 minutes until apples are tender but crisp. Keep warm. Beat eggs with milk in bowl. Melt remaining 2 tablespoons butter in 9-inch omelet pan. When sizzling, add egg mixture. Slide metal spatula around edge of pan, carefully lifting egg so uncooked portion can flow underneath. Cook until set; transfer to warm platter. Top with apple mixture. Serve immediately.

Lunch for Two

Makes 2 servings
Preparation Time: 20 minutes

- 1 cup frozen French-style green beans, thawed
- ¼ cup mushrooms
- ¼ cup chopped onion
- 2 tablespoons butter
- 4 eggs
- ¼ cup water
- ½ teaspoon salt
- ½ cup plain yogurt
- ⅛ teaspoon dried dillweed
  Dash garlic powder
- 1 teaspoon minced chives
  Freshly ground pepper, optional

Sauté beans, mushrooms and onion in 1 tablespoon butter in skillet until tender; set aside. Beat eggs, water and salt in bowl with fork. Heat remaining 1 tablespoon butter in 10-inch omelet pan; pour in eggs. Slide metal spatula around edge of pan, lifting egg mixture carefully so uncooked eggs can flow underneath. Spread bean mixture over half of omelet while top is moist and creamy-looking. Fold omelet in half with pancake turner; transfer to platter. Mix yogurt, dillweed and garlic powder; pour over omelet. Sprinkle with chives and freshly ground pepper, if desired. Serve immediately.

Welsh Rarebit

Makes 4 to 6 servings
Preparation Time: 15 minutes

- ¼ **cup butter**
- ¼ **cup flour**
- 2 **cups milk**
- 1 **teaspoon Worcestershire sauce**
- 1 **teaspoon dry mustard**
- ½ **teaspoon salt**
- ⅛ **teaspoon cayenne pepper**
- 1 **pound shredded Cheddar cheese** *or* **sharp process American cheese**
  Toast triangles
  Paprika

Melt butter in 2-quart saucepan. Add flour; cook, stirring until bubbly. Add next 5 ingredients; stir until thickened. Add cheese, stirring until melted. Do *not* overcook. Pour over toast triangles; sprinkle with paprika. Serve immediately.

Athenian Omelet

Makes 1 serving
Preparation Time: 15 minutes

- 2 **eggs**
- ⅓ **cup crumbled feta cheese**
- ⅓ **cup chopped tomato**
- ⅓ **cup thinly sliced green onion**
- 1 **tablespoon grated Parmesan cheese**
  Dash ground black pepper
- 1 **tablespoon butter**

Beat eggs in bowl; add next 5 ingredients. Melt butter in 8-inch omelet pan over medium heat. When butter sizzles, pour egg mixture in pan. Push cooked portion of egg mixture toward center so uncooked portion can flow to bottom of pan. Cook 3 to 4 minutes; turn; brown other side. Remove from heat; invert large dinner plate over frying pan. Turn over; slide omelet back into pan. Cook 1 minute. Serve immediately.

Frozen Cheese Soufflé

Makes 4 servings
Preparation Time: 30 minutes; freeze overnight; 70 minutes to bake

- ¼ **cup butter**
- ¼ **cup flour**
- ¾ **cup half-and-half**
- ¼ **cup dry white wine**
- ½ **teaspoon salt**
- ⅛ **teaspoon ground white pepper**
- 1½ **cups shredded natural Swiss cheese, lightly packed**
- 6 **eggs, separated**
- ¼ **teaspoon cream of tartar**

Melt butter in 2-quart saucepan. Add flour; cook, stirring until bubbly. Do *not* brown flour. Stir in next 5 ingredients; cook, stirring over low heat until cheese melts; remove from heat. Beat yolks in bowl until thick; stir into cheese mixture. Beat whites with cream of tartar in bowl until stiff but not dry. Fold 1 cup whites into sauce, using rubber spatula. Fold in remaining whites; pour into 1½-quart freezer-to-oven casserole. Cover; freeze overnight. Preheat oven to 300°. Remove cover from casserole; bake 70 minutes. Serve immediately.

Hoppel Poppel

Makes 2 servings
Preparation Time: 15 minutes

- ⅓ **cup thinly sliced potatoes**
- 1 **tablespoon butter**
- ⅛ **teaspoon salt**
  Dash ground white pepper
- ⅓ **cup diced salami** *or* **ham**
- 1 **tablespoon minced chives**
- 3 **eggs**
  Parsley sprigs

Sauté potatoes in butter in 8-inch omelet pan until lightly browned and tender. Sprinkle with salt and pepper. Add ham and chives; heat through. Beat eggs in bowl with fork; pour over ham and potatoes. Lift cooked portion of egg mixture at edges of pan with metal spatula so uncooked portion can flow to bottom. When eggs are set, invert dinner plate over skillet and turn over. Slide back into pan to brown other side. Garnish with parsley; serve immediately.

Zucchini Frittata

Makes 2 servings
Preparation Time: 15 minutes

- 2 tablespoons butter
- 1½ cups thinly sliced zucchini coins, cut in fourths
- 1 small onion, chopped
- ⅛ teaspoon dried dillweed
- ⅛ teaspoon salt
- ⅛ teaspoon ground black pepper
- 4 eggs
- ½ cup shredded mozzarella cheese, lightly packed
- ½ cup plain yogurt
- 1 tablespoon minced chives

Melt 1 tablespoon butter in 8-inch skillet. Sauté next 5 ingredients until onion is translucent. Remove; keep warm. Melt remaining 1 tablespoon butter in skillet over medium heat. Beat eggs lightly; pour into pan. Slide metal spatula around edge of pan, carefully lifting eggs so uncooked portion can flow underneath. Cook just until bottom is golden and eggs are partially set. Sprinkle cheese over eggs; top with zucchini mixture. Slide onto plate; top with yogurt and sprinkle with chives. Serve immediately.

Quiche Lorraine

Makes 6 servings
Preparation Time: 30 minutes; 45 minutes to bake; 10 minutes to set

- ¾ pound bacon *or* 1 pound bulk pork sausage
- 1 9-inch unbaked piecrust
- ½ cup chopped onion
- 1 tablespoon flour
- 4 eggs
- 2 cups shredded natural Swiss cheese, lightly packed
- 1½ cups half-and-half *or* evaporated milk
- ½ teaspoon salt
- ¼ teaspoon ground black pepper
- ⅛ teaspoon ground nutmeg
  Paprika

Preheat oven to 375°. Cook bacon in skillet over medium heat until crisp. Cool; crumble; reserve ¼ cup. Sprinkle remaining bacon into piecrust. Remove all fat except 2 tablespoons from skillet. Sauté onion until golden; sprinkle over bacon. Sprinkle flour over bacon and onion. Beat eggs lightly in bowl. Add next 5 ingredients; pour into piecrust. Sprinkle with reserved ¼ cup bacon and paprika. Bake 35 to 45 minutes. Let stand 10 minutes before serving.

Chicken Liver Omelet

Makes 2 servings
Preparation Time: 20 minutes

- ½ pound chicken livers
- 1 tablespoon lemon juice
- ¼ cup butter
- ½ teaspoon salt
- ½ teaspoon dried oregano
- ¼ teaspoon ground black pepper
- ¼ cup thinly sliced onion
- ½ cup chopped tomato
- 4 eggs
- 1 tablespoon milk
- ½ cup plain yogurt
- 1 teaspoon minced chives

Remove fat and white tissue from livers; discard. Cut livers in bite-size pieces; sprinkle with lemon juice. Melt 2 tablespoons butter in skillet over medium heat. Add livers; sprinkle with ¼ teaspoon salt, oregano and pepper. Cook about 3 minutes, stirring occasionally. Add onion; cook 2 minutes. Add tomato; cook 3 to 4 minutes. Remove from heat; cover and keep warm. Beat eggs, milk and remaining ¼ teaspoon salt in bowl. Melt remaining 2 tablespoons butter in 8-inch omelet pan over medium heat. Add egg mixture, pushing cooked portions at edge of pan toward center so uncooked portion can flow to bottom. Cook 3 to 4 minutes. Arrange chicken liver mixture down center of omelet. Cover with both sides of omelet. Slide onto serving plate; spoon yogurt over top and sprinkle with chives. Serve immediately.

Skillet Scramble

Makes 2 servings
Preparation Time: 15 minutes

- 2 tablespoons butter
- 1½ cups frozen hash brown potatoes, thawed
- ¼ teaspoon salt
- 4 slices bacon, cooked and crumbled
- 4 eggs
- 2 tablespoons half-and-half *or* milk
- ½ cup shredded Monterey Jack, brick *or* Muenster cheese
- ⅛ teaspoon water

Melt butter in 10-inch skillet over medium heat. Add potatoes; sprinkle with salt. Cook 2 to 3 minutes; sprinkle with bacon. Beat eggs with half-and-half in bowl. Pour over potatoes; cook until eggs are almost set. Sprinkle with cheese. Add water to pan; cover; cook 1 minute or until cheese melts. Serve immediately.

Brunch

Brunch Benedict

Makes 2 servings
Preparation Time: 15 minutes

  2 eggs, poached
  2 English muffins, split and toasted
  4 thin slices ham
  4 canned asparagus spears *or* 4 fresh asparagus
    spears, cooked and drained
    Paprika
  1 pitted ripe olive, cut in 4 thin slices
  2 parsley sprigs
    Hollandaise Sauce

Make Hollandaise Sauce; keep warm. Poach eggs. Place 2 muffin halves on each plate; top with ham and asparagus. Set hot, drained poached egg on top of each serving. Top with sauce; sprinkle with paprika. Place 2 olive slices and parsley sprig on each serving.

Hollandaise Sauce

  ¼ cup butter *or* margarine
  2 egg yolks
  2 tablespoons plain yogurt *or* fresh lemon juice
    Dash ground white pepper

Combine first 3 ingredients in 1-quart saucepan. Cook, stirring, over low heat until mixture thickens. Stir in pepper.

Cheese Blintzes

Makes 4 servings
Preparation Time: 45 minutes; 2 hours to chill crepe batter

 12 Whole Wheat Crêpes
  1 cup cottage cheese
  ¼ cup dairy sour cream
  2 tablespoons butter
    Sour cream
    Snipped chives

Prepare Crêpes. Mix cottage cheese and sour cream. Place about 1½ tablespoons cheese mixture in center of each Whole Wheat Crêpe. Fold two edges toward center, then fold remaining two edges toward center again. (Crêpes may be refrigerated at this point and heated later.) Melt butter in 10-inch skillet. Sauté crepes until brown on all sides. Serve garnished with dollops of sour cream topped with chives.

Whole Wheat Crêpes

Makes 10 to 12 crêpes

  3 eggs
  1 cup milk
  ⅔ cup whole wheat flour
  ¼ teaspoon salt
  2 tablespoons butter, melted

Beat eggs and milk in bowl. Add flour and salt; beat with whisk until smooth. Refrigerate 2 hours *or* overnight. Brush 8-inch omelet pan or crêpe pan with a little butter. Warm pan over medium heat. Pour about 2 tablespoons batter into pan; tilt quickly to coat bottom evenly. Cook until crêpe is dry and firm in center. (Crêpes should be golden but not brown.) Do *not* turn. Stack crêpes between sheets of wax paper. Brush pan with a little butter after every other crêpe, if necessary.

Chicken Divan Crêpes

Makes 4 servings
Preparation Time: 20 minutes; 20 minutes to bake

  1 cup plain yogurt
  1 11-ounce can condensed Cheddar cheese soup
  ¼ teaspoon Dijon mustard
    Dash Worcestershire sauce
  8 broccoli spears, cooked and drained *or* 2 10-ounce
    packages frozen broccoli spears, cooked and
    drained
  8 Crêpes (see page 29)
  2½ cups cooked chicken julienne strips
  1 cup grated sharp Cheddar cheese

Preheat oven to 350°. Stir yogurt in small saucepan until creamy. Add soup and mustard; blend well. Place over medium heat, stirring constantly, until mixture begins to bubble. Remove from heat; stir in Worcestershire sauce. Spread ¼ cup sauce evenly over bottom of shallow 9 by 13-inch baking pan. Place 1 cooked broccoli spear in center of each crêpe. Mix ½ cup sauce with chicken strips; spoon over broccoli spears; sprinkle each with 1 tablespoon cheese. Fold one side over to cover most of filling; fold other side over the first side. Place in pan; pour remaining sauce over center of crêpes. Cover; bake 15 minutes. Uncover; sprinkle remaining cheese over top of crêpes. Bake 3 to 5 minutes.

Florentine Crêpes

Makes 4 servings
Preparation Time: 30 minutes; 20 minutes to bake

- 2 10-ounce packages frozen chopped spinach
- ¼ cup olive or vegetable oil
- ½ cup thinly sliced green onion
- 2 cups diced cooked chicken
- ½ teaspoon salt
- ½ teaspoon dried dill weed
- ¼ teaspoon dried mint leaves, crushed
- ⅛ teaspoon ground white pepper
- 6 ounces feta cheese, crumbled
- 1 tablespoon chopped parsley
- 1 teaspoon grated Parmesan cheese
- 1 egg, lightly beaten
- 8 Crepes
- 2 teaspoons butter, melted
  Béchamel Sauce

Preheat oven to 375°. Grease 9 by 13-inch baking pan. Cook spinach according to package directions; drain. Press out all excess water. Heat oil in 10-inch skillet. Sauté onion 2 minutes. Add chicken; sauté 2 minutes. Add spinach and next 4 ingredients; sauté 3 minutes. Remove from heat; add next 4 ingredients; mix well. Place about 3 tablespoons filling down center of each crêpe; fold both sides of crêpe over filling. Place seam-side-down in pan; brush with melted butter. Cover; bake 15 to 20 minutes. Serve immediately with Béchamel Sauce.

Note: Remaining 6 crepes can be stacked between sheets of wax paper, tightly wrapped with foil and frozen for another use.

Béchamel Sauce

Makes approximately 1 cup sauce

- 2 tablespoons butter
- 2 tablespoons flour
- 1 cup milk or half-and-half
- 2 tablespoons dry white wine
- ⅛ teaspoon salt
- ⅛ teaspoon ground white pepper

Melt butter in 1-quart saucepan over medium heat. Add flour; stir until bubbly. Add milk; stirring until thickened, about 5 minutes. Stir in wine, salt and pepper; heat to serving temperature.

Crêpes

Makes 14

- 2 eggs
- 1 cup plus 2 tablespoons milk
- 1 cup flour
- 1 tablespoon vegetable oil
- ⅛ teaspoon salt
- 2 tablespoons melted butter

Beat eggs in a medium bowl. Add milk, flour, oil and salt. Beat again until batter is smooth. Cover and refrigerate 2 hours. Preheat a 6 or 8-inch omelet pan. Brush with a little of the butter. Pour about 3 tablespoons batter into pan and cook 2 to 3 minutes, rotating pan as batter is poured. Cook until lightly browned on bottom. Loosen edges with spatula and gently lift crêpe. Stack between pieces of waxed paper. Keep covered.

Fruited Chicken Mélange

Makes 4 servings
Preparation Time: 20 minutes

- 2 tablespoons vegetable oil
- 2 whole chicken breasts, boned, skinned and cut in thin strips
- ½ teaspoon salt
- ⅛ teaspoon ground white pepper
- 1 teaspoon minced crystallized ginger
  Dash ground cinnamon
- 2 firm pears, cut in wedges
- 3 tablespoons Madeira wine
- 1 tablespoon light brown sugar, firmly packed
- 2 large apples, cut in wedges
- 3 tablespoons chopped dates
- 3 tablespoons golden raisins
  Hot cooked rice
- 2 tablespoons toasted slivered almonds

Heat oil in large skillet over medium heat. Sauté chicken, stirring 2 to 3 minutes or until light golden. Add next 4 ingredients; toss to mix well. Stir in pear wedges, Madeira and brown sugar; cover; simmer 5 minutes. Add apple wedges, dates and raisins; cover; simmer 2 minutes. Serve over hot cooked rice; sprinkle with almonds.

Asparagus Quiche

Makes 6 servings
Preparation Time: 15 minutes; 60 minutes to bake

- 1½ cups shredded Swiss cheese, lightly packed
- 1 tablespoon flour
- 1 9-inch unbaked piecrust
- 1 10½-ounce can cut asparagus, drained
- 1 4-ounce can sliced mushrooms, drained
- 4 eggs
- 1½ cups half-and-half
- ½ teaspoon salt
- ¼ teaspoon ground white pepper
- ⅛ teaspoon grated nutmeg
  Paprika

Preheat oven to 350°. Mix cheese with flour; spread in crust. Top with asparagus and mushrooms. Beat eggs lightly in bowl; stir in next 4 ingredients. Pour over asparagus mixture; sprinkle with paprika. Bake 1 hour or until a knife inserted in center comes out clean. Let stand 5 minutes before serving.

Note: One 10-ounce package frozen chopped spinach *or* broccoli, cooked according to package directions and drained, can be substituted for asparagus.

Gazpacho Macaroni Salad

Makes 6 to 8 servings
Preparation Time: 20 minutes

- 2 cups uncooked macaroni
- 1 10-ounce package frozen peas
- 3 medium-size tomatoes, peeled and chopped
- 1 cup chopped celery
- 1 medium-size cucumber, diced
- 1 green pepper, cored and chopped
- 5 green onions, thinly sliced
- 6 ounces salami, cubed
- ¼ cup finely chopped parsley
- ⅓ cup olive oil
- ¼ cup wine vinegar
- 1 teaspoon salt
- ½ teaspoon Worcestershire sauce
  Hot pepper sauce to taste
- 1 clove garlic, pressed
  Lettuce cups
  Ripe olives

Cook macaroni according to package directions; drain; rinse in cold water; drain again. Place peas in bowl; cover with boiling water; let stand 1 to 2 minutes; drain. Put macaroni, peas and next 7 ingredients in bowl. Put next 6 ingredients in covered container; shake well.

Pour over macaroni mixture; toss lightly. Serve in lettuce cups garnished with olives.

Note: Salad may be mixed with dressing and chilled 3 hours. Toss again before serving.

Best-Ever Beef 'n Biscuits

Makes 3 servings
Preparation Time: 30 minutes; 20 minutes to bake

- ¾ pound ground beef
- ¾ cup chopped celery
- ¾ cup shredded Cheddar cheese, lightly packed
- 1 tablespoon chopped green chilies
- ½ teaspoon salt
- 1 10-ounce can refrigerated buttermilk *or* country-style biscuits
- 1¼ cups crushed corn chips
- ½ cup dairy sour cream
- 1 small tomato, chopped

Preheat oven to 375°. Brown beef in skillet, stirring to break up meat. Add celery during last few minutes; remove from heat; drain off fat. Stir in next 3 ingredients. Separate biscuits; place on chips on countertop. Roll each to 6-inch circle, coating both sides with chips. Spoon about ½ cup meat filling on center of 5 rolled biscuits; cover with remaining 5 biscuits. Press edges with fork to seal. Bake 18 to 20 minutes. Serve warm, topped with dollop of sour cream and sprinkling of chopped tomato.

Broccoli Noodle Soufflé

Makes 4 servings
Preparation Time: 20 minutes; 25 minutes to bake

- 2 cups medium-wide egg noodles
- 1 10-ounce package frozen chopped broccoli
- ¼ cup boiling water
- 7 eggs, separated
- ½ cup grated Parmesan cheese
- ½ teaspoon salt
- ¼ teaspoon ground black pepper
- ⅛ teaspoon cream of tartar

Preheat oven to 350°. Grease 1½-quart baking dish *or* soufflé dish. Cook noodles according to package directions; drain; cool. Cook broccoli in boiling water 5 minutes; drain well; cool. Combine noodles, broccoli, egg yolks, cheese, salt and pepper in bowl. Beat whites until frothy; add cream of tartar; beat until stiff but not dry. Fold into broccoli mixture; pour into dish. Bake 20 to 25 minutes.

Gazpacho Macaroni Salad, this page

Brunch

Trio Cheese Bake

Makes 4 to 6 servings
Preparation Time: 30 minutes; 65 minutes to bake

 ½ 17½-ounce package frozen puff pastry
 5 eggs
 1 tablespoon minced chives
 ¼ teaspoon dried oregano
 1 cup crumbled feta cheese
 1 cup ricotta cheese
 ¼ cup grated Parmesan cheese
 1 teaspoon milk

Preheat oven to 350°. Grease 6 by 10-inch baking pan. Thaw one sheet pastry at room temperature 20 minutes. Unfold; cut in half. Roll one piece to 10 by 14-inch rectangle on floured surface. Fit into bottom and up sides of baking pan. Roll remaining piece into 7 by 10-inch rectangle; set aside. Beat 4 eggs with chives and oregano in bowl. Blend in all cheeses; mix well. Pour into pastry-lined baking dish; cover with remaining pastry sheet. Beat remaining egg with milk in bowl; brush top of pastry. Prick holes in top with tines of fork. Bake 50 to 55 minutes; let stand 10 minutes before serving.

Sunnyside Skillet

Makes 4 servings
Preparation Time: 40 minutes

 ½ cup thinly sliced green onions
 ½ cup chopped celery
 2 tablespoons butter
 3 cups cooked white rice
 1 teaspoon salt
   Few drops liquid hot pepper sauce
 1 cup shredded Cheddar cheese, lightly packed
 4 eggs
 8 slices bacon, cooked, drained, crumbled
 1 tomato, chopped

Sauté onion and celery in butter in 10-inch skillet until onions are tender, but not brown. Add next 3 ingredients; cook until rice is heated through. Stir in ¾ cup cheese; mix well. Make 4 indentations in rice with back of spoon; break egg into each indentation. Sprinkle with remaining cheese, bacon and tomato. Cover; cook 3 to 5 minutes or until cheese melts and eggs are cooked. Serve immediately.

Reuben Casserole

Makes 6 servings
Preparation Time: 30 minutes; 20 minutes to bake

 1 27-ounce can sauerkraut, drained
 ½ teaspoon caraway seeds
 ½ cup thousand island salad dressing
 10 ounces thinly sliced corned beef
 2 cups shredded Swiss cheese, lightly packed
 1 4½-ounce can refrigerated buttermilk biscuits
 ½ cup crushed rye crackers
 2 tablespoons butter, softened

Preheat oven to 245°. Spread sauerkraut in 9 by 13-inch baking pan. Sprinkle with caraway seed. Cover with dressing. Top with corned beef and cheese. Bake 15 minutes. Separate and place each biscuit on crushed crackers. Roll each into 4-inch circle, coating both sides with crackers. Arrange over casserole. Bake 15 to 20 minutes. Brush biscuit tops with butter before serving.

Hot Turkey Salad

Makes 6 servings
Preparation Time: 25 minutes

 2 tablespoons butter
 2 cups chopped cooked turkey
 ½ cup chopped celery
 1 cup dairy sour cream
 ½ cup mayonnaise
 ¼ cup sweet pickle relish
 ¼ cup chopped pimiento, drained
 1 tablespoon chopped chives
 2 teaspoons salt
 ⅛ teaspoon ground white pepper
 2 hard-cooked eggs, chopped
 6 slices bread, toasted
 ⅓ cup slivered almonds, toasted

Melt butter in 2-quart saucepan over medium heat. Sauté turkey and celery 5 minutes. Blend sour cream and mayonnaise in small bowl. Stir in next 6 ingredients; add to turkey mixture. Cook over low heat to warm through. Serve hot on toast. Sprinkle with almonds before serving.

Beef Zucchini Skillet

Makes 4 servings
Preparation Time: 20 minutes; 1¾ hours to cook

- 2 tablespoons butter
- 1 tablespoon vegetable oil
- 1 pound lean beef stew meat, cut in 1-inch cubes
- 1 medium-size onion, chopped
- ¼ cup chopped celery
- 1 small clove garlic, pressed
- 1 teaspoon salt
- ⅛ teaspoon ground black pepper
- ½ teaspoon dried oregano
- ½ cup tomato puree
- 1 cup beef broth
- 1 cup water
- 6 cups sliced zucchini

Heat butter and oil in large kettle over medium heat. Add next 7 ingredients; brown meat on all sides, stirring occasionally. Stir in tomato puree, beef broth and water; bring to boil. Reduce heat; cover; simmer 1½ hours or until meat is almost tender. Stir in zucchini; bring to boil. Cover; simmer 10 minutes or until zucchini is tender.

Potluck Skillet Supper

Makes 4 servings
Preparation Time: 45 minutes

- 1 pound lean ground beef
- 2 eggs, lightly beaten
- 1¼ cups milk
- ½ cup fine dry bread crumbs
- 3 tablespoons minced onion
- 1½ teaspoons salt
- ½ teaspoon dry mustard
- ¼ cup flour
- 2 tablespoons vegetable oil
- 1 10½-ounce can condensed cream of mushroom soup
- 1 10-ounce package frozen mixed vegetables
- 1 3-ounce can French-fried onion rings

Mix beef, eggs, ½ cup milk, bread crumbs, onion, 1 teaspoon salt and mustard in bowl. Shape into 24 meatballs; roll in flour. Heat oil in 10-inch skillet. Brown meatballs over medium heat, about 10 minutes. Reduce heat; arrange meatballs around edge of pan. Combine soup and remaining ¾ cup milk; pour into skillet. Place vegetables in center of skillet. Sprinkle with remaining ½ teaspoon salt. Cover; simmer 15 minutes. Sprinkle with onion rings before serving.

Lamb Shank Pilaf

Makes 4 servings
Preparation Time: 30 minutes; 1½ hours to cook

- 4 lamb shanks or 2 pounds lamb, fat trimmed
- 1 tablespoon lemon juice
- 2 teaspoons salt
- ½ teaspoon ground black pepper
- 1 clove garlic, pressed
- 5 tablespoons butter
- ½ cup chopped onion
- ½ cup chopped celery
- 2 cups hot water
- 1 16-ounce can tomatoes with juice, cut up
- 1 teaspoon sugar
- 1 cup uncooked rice
- 1 cup plain yogurt, optional

Preheat oven to 350°. Sprinkle lamb with lemon juice, 1 teaspoon salt and pepper. Brown evenly on all sides with garlic in 1 tablespoon butter in large kettle over medium heat. Add onion and celery during last few minutes of browning. Add water; bring to boil. Cover; simmer 1 hour. Add tomatoes and sugar; bring to boil. Stir in rice and remaining 1 teaspoon salt. Bring to boil; cover; bake 30 minutes. Heat remaining 4 tablespoons butter in small skillet over medium heat until brown. Pour over rice and lamb; stir gently to coat rice with butter. Serve yogurt over rice, if desired.

One-Pot Veal Parmigiana

Makes 4 servings
Preparation Time: 30 minutes

- 4 veal steaks or chops (1 to 1½ pounds)
- 2 tablespoons butter
- 3 cups water
- 1 6-ounce can tomato paste
- 1 teaspoon dried Italian herbs
- 1 teaspoon salt
- ⅛ teaspoon ground black pepper
- ½ pound uncooked spaghetti
- ½ pound thinly sliced mozzarella cheese

Brown veal on both sides in butter in large kettle, 4 to 5 minutes per side. Remove; set aside. Add next 5 ingredients; bring to boil. Gradually stir in spaghetti; bring to boil, stirring occasionally. Cover; simmer 6 minutes. Arrange veal on top of spaghetti. Top with cheese. Cover; simmer 5 minutes or until cheese melts and spaghetti is tender.

Skillet

15-Minute Skillet Casserole

Makes 4 to 6 servings
Preparation Time: 15 minutes

- 1 16-ounce can baked beans
- 1 pound frankfurters, cut diagonally in 1-inch pieces
- 1 cup chopped onion
- ⅓ cup catsup
- ¼ cup light brown sugar, firmly packed
- 1 teaspoon chili powder

Mix all ingredients in 2-quart saucepan; bring to boil. Reduce heat; simmer 10 minutes.

Pork Chops Oregano

Makes 4 servings
Preparation Time: 1 hour

- 1 tablespoon olive oil
- 1 tablespoon butter
- 4 ½-inch thick pork loin *or* rib chops
- 4 medium-size potatoes, peeled, cut in ¼-inch thick crosswise slices
- 1 medium-size onion, sliced lengthwise
- ½ teaspoon salt
- ⅛ teaspoon ground black pepper
- 1 teaspoon dried oregano
- 2 teaspoons lemon juice
- 1 green pepper, cored, quartered
- 1 tomato, cut in wedges

Heat oil and butter in 10-inch skillet with cover over medium heat. Brown chops on one side; turn; arrange potatoes and onion around and on top of chops. Sprinkle with next 4 ingredients; cover; cook over low heat 30 minutes. Add green pepper; cook 5 minutes. Garnish with tomato wedges.

Sweet-Sour Skillet

Makes 4 servings
Preparation Time: 25 minutes

- 1 pound bulk Italian sausage, broken in 1-inch pieces
- 1 teaspoon dried oregano
- ⅓ cup light brown sugar, firmly packed
- ⅓ cup cider vinegar
- 6 cups shredded cabbage
- 2 large red apples, cored, sliced

Put sausage in 10-inch skillet over low heat. Add oregano; cook until sausage is browned; drain off fat. Stir in brown sugar and vinegar; mix well. Add cabbage. Bring to boil; cover; simmer 5 minutes. Stir; simmer 5 minutes. Arrange apple slices on top of cabbage. Cover; cook 2 to 3 minutes.

Skillet Meat Loaf

Makes 4 to 6 servings
Preparation Time: 20 minutes; 65 minutes to cook

- 1 pound lean ground beef
- ¼ cup catsup
- ¼ cup milk
- ½ cup fine dry bread crumbs
- 2 tablespoons minced parsley
- 2 tablespoons instant minced onion
- 2 eggs, lightly beaten
- ¼ cup grated Parmesan cheese
- 1 teaspoon Worcestershire sauce
- 1½ teaspoons salt
- ¼ teaspoon ground black pepper
  Flour
- 1 teaspoon vegetable oil
- 1 tablespoon butter
- 4 medium-size potatoes, peeled, quartered lengthwise
- 1 teaspoon chopped chives
- ⅛ teaspoon ground black pepper
- 1 10-ounce package frozen peas, thawed

Mix first 9 ingredients with 1 teaspoon salt and ¼ teaspoon pepper in large bowl. Shape into 2 5-inch long loaves. Roll each in flour, coating generously. Heat oil and butter in 10-inch skillet over medium-high heat or in electric skillet heated to 350°. Brown loaves evenly on three sides, turning carefully. Turn on last side; place in center of pan. Arrange potatoes around loaves; sprinkle with chives, remaining ½ teaspoon salt and ⅛ teaspoon pepper. Reduce heat; cover; cook 1 hour, carefully turning meat and stirring potatoes every 15 minutes. Sprinkle peas over potatoes. Cover; cook 5 minutes.

Spicy Sausage Serenade

Makes 4 to 6 servings
Preparation Time: 30 minutes

- 1 pound bulk Italian sausage, broken into 1-inch pieces
- 1 tablespoon butter
- 1 large onion, chopped
- 1 cup chopped celery
- ½ teaspoon salt
- ¼ teaspoon dried rosemary
- ¼ teaspoon dried marjoram
- 1 17-ounce can lima beans
- 1 1-pound can tomatoes

Brown sausage in 10-inch skillet over low heat, about 10 minutes. Remove from heat; drain off fat. Add butter, onion and celery; sauté until onions are translucent. Add next 5 ingredients; bring to boil. Cover; simmer 10 minutes.

Pork Chops Oregano, this page
Sweet-Sour Skillet, this page

Skillet

Chicken Noodle Skillet Dinner

Makes 4 servings
Preparation Time: 30 minutes; 45 minutes to cook

- 2 tablespoons butter
- 1 tablespoon vegetable oil
- 1 3-pound broiler-fryer chicken, cut in serving pieces
- 1½ cups finely chopped celery
- 1 cup finely chopped onion
- ¼ cup shredded carrot
- 1 small clove garlic, pressed
- 1 teaspoon salt
- ¼ teaspoon ground white pepper
- ½ teaspoon dried tarragon leaves
- 1½ cups diced tomato
- ¼ cup tomato puree
- 1 chicken bouillon cube
- ½ cup water
- 1 pound curly egg noodles, cooked, drained
  Freshly grated Parmesan cheese

Heat butter and oil in 10-inch skillet over medium heat. Brown chicken pieces, skin-side-down until golden. Turn; brown other side. Remove from pan; set aside. Add next 6 ingredients to pan drippings; sauté until celery and onion are tender. Add next 5 ingredients; bring to boil. Reduce heat to low; simmer 3 minutes. Arrange chicken pieces over vegetables. Cover; simmer 30 minutes. Arrange noodles in center of large serving platter; place chicken around noodles. Pour cooked vegetables and sauce over noodles. Sprinkle with cheese; serve immediately.

Note: Chicken will not spatter when it is cooked if the pieces are blotted dry with paper towels.

Country-Style Chicken

Makes 4 servings
Preparation Time: 1¼ hours

- 1 2 to 2½-pound broiler-fryer chicken, cut in serving pieces
- 1 teaspoon salt
- ¼ teaspoon ground black pepper
- 3 tablespoons butter
- 1 tablespoon vegetable oil
- 1 16-ounce can tomatoes with juice, cut up
- ¼ cup tomato paste
- ⅛ teaspoon dried tarragon
- 1 chicken bouillon cube
- 1½ cups boiling water
- 2 cups corkscrew rotini macaroni
  Grated Parmesan cheese

Sprinkle chicken with salt and pepper. Heat butter and oil in large kettle over medium-high heat. Brown chicken 7 to 8 minutes per side. Stir in next 3 ingredients; bring to boil. Cover; simmer 35 minutes. Dissolve bouillon cube in boiling water. Add to kettle; bring to boil. Stir in rotini; bring to boil. Reduce heat; cook, uncovered, 10 minutes or until rotini is tender. Serve immediately with Parmesan cheese.

Anchovy Pot Roast

Makes 4 to 6 servings
Preparation Time: 20 minutes; 3 hours to cook

- 2 to 3 pound boneless *or* bone-in chuck blade pot roast
- 2 teaspoons vegetable oil
- 1 teaspoon salt
- ¼ teaspoon ground black pepper
- 2 cups hot beef broth
- 2 onions, chopped
- 1 stalk celery, chopped
- 4 anchovy fillets, chopped
- 10 whole allspice
- 1 bay leaf
- 2 tablespoons vinegar
- 1 tablespoon molasses
- ½ pound mostaccioli macaroni
- 1 20-ounce package frozen peas
  Grated Parmesan cheese

Brown roast on both sides in oil in large kettle over medium heat. Sprinkle with salt and pepper. Add next 8 ingredients; bring to boil. Cover; simmer 2½ to 3 hours or until meat is tender. Remove meat; keep warm. Strain broth; add enough water to measure 2½ cups. Bring to boil. Stir in mostaccioli. Cook, uncovered, stirring occasionally, 10 minutes until mostaccioli is tender. Stir in peas during last few minutes; heat through. Pass grated Parmesan cheese for mostaccioli.

Dilled Beef Stew Skillet

Makes 4 servings
Preparation Time: 15 minutes; 1½ hours to cook

- 1½ pounds lean beef stew meat, cut in 1-inch cubes
- 3 tablespoons flour
- 1½ teaspoons salt
- ¼ teaspoon ground black pepper
- 1 tablespoon vegetable oil
- 2 cups hot beef broth
- 1 bay leaf
- ¾ teaspoon dried dillweed
- 1½ cups water
- 1 8-ounce can tomato puree *or* sauce
- 1 cup uncooked rice
- 2 cups plain yogurt, optional

Roll meat in flour mixed with salt and pepper. Heat oil in 12-inch skillet over medium heat. Brown meat evenly on all sides. Add next 3 ingredients; cover; simmer 1 hour. Add water and tomato puree; bring to boil; stir in rice. Bring to a boil; reduce heat; cover; simmer 25 minutes or until all liquid is absorbed. Spoon ½ cup yogurt over each serving, if desired.

Pork-Cauliflower Stew

Makes 4 servings
Preparation Time: 20 minutes; 1 hour to cook

- 1 pound lean pork, cut in 1-inch cubes
- 1 medium-size onion, chopped
- 1 clove garlic, minced
- ¼ cup butter
- 3 cups hot water
- ½ cup tomato sauce
- 1 teaspoon salt
- ¼ teaspoon ground white pepper
- 1 small head cauliflower, cut into flowerets
  Lemon wedges

Brown pork, onion and garlic in butter in large kettle over medium heat. Add next 4 ingredients; bring to boil. Cover; simmer 45 minutes. Add cauliflower; bring to boil. Cook 15 minutes or until cauliflower is tender. Serve with lemon wedges.

Pork Chops Frijoles

Makes 4 servings
Preparation Time: 50 minutes

- 4 ½-inch thick loin *or* rib pork chops
- ½ teaspoon salt
- ⅛ teaspoon ground black pepper
- 1 tablespoon vegetable oil
- 1½ cups chopped celery
- ½ cup chopped onion
- 1 clove garlic, pressed
- ½ cup tomato sauce
- 1 1-pound can black-eyed peas, drained
- 1 teaspoon chili powder
- ½ teaspoon dried oregano

Sprinkle chops with salt and pepper. Brown on both sides in hot oil in 10-inch skillet. Remove; set aside. Sauté celery, onion and garlic in drippings until onion is translucent. Add next 4 ingredients; bring to boil. Arrange chops on top. Cover; cook 20 minutes.

Pork Hocks

Makes 4 servings
Preparation Time: 2½ hours

- 4 slices bacon, chopped
- 4 pounds pork hocks
- 1 clove garlic, minced
- 1 cup chopped onion
- 1 cup chopped celery
- 3 cups hot water
- 1 teaspoon salt
- ½ teaspoon dried oregano
- ¼ teaspoon ground black pepper
- 1 6-ounce can tomato paste
- 2 1-pound cans black-eyed peas, drained

Brown bacon, pork hocks and garlic in large kettle over medium heat. Add onion and celery during last few minutes of browning. Add next 4 ingredients; bring to boil. Cover; simmer 1½ hours. Add tomato paste and black-eyed peas; bring to boil. Boil, uncovered, 3 minutes. Cover; simmer 30 minutes.

Short Ribs and Dumplings

Makes 4 servings
Preparation Time: 30 minutes; 3 hours to cook

- 3 pounds beef short ribs, cut in pieces, excess fat removed
- 2 tablespoons vegetable oil
- 2 medium-size onions, chopped
- 1 cup chopped celery
- 2 cloves garlic, pressed
- 4 cups hot water
- 1 16-ounce can tomatoes with juice, cut up
- 2 beef bouillon cubes
- 4 teaspoons Worcestershire sauce
- 2 bay leaves
- 1 teaspoon salt
- ¼ teaspoon ground black pepper
- 1 pound carrots, cut in 1-inch pieces
- 1½ cups biscuit mix
- 1 teaspoon ground savory
- ½ cup milk

Brown ribs on all sides in oil in large kettle. Add onion, celery and garlic during last few minutes of browning. Add next 7 ingredients; bring to boil. Cover; simmer 1½ hours, stirring several times. Add carrots; bring to boil. Cover; simmer 1 hour. Combine biscuit mix and savory in bowl. Stir in milk. Bring stew to boil again; drop 8 tablespoons of dough into stew. Cook 5 minutes; cover; cook 15 minutes.

Skillet

Basque-Style Veal Skillet

Makes 4 servings
Preparation Time: 15 minutes; 1 hour to cook

- 1 pound veal stew meat
- 1 cup chopped onion
- ¼ cup butter
- 1 16-ounce can stewed tomatoes
- 3 cups water
- 1 tablespoon parsley flakes
- 1 teaspoon salt
- 1 teaspoon garlic powder
- ½ teaspoon dried tarragon
- ¼ teaspoon ground black pepper
- 2 cups rotini macaroni
- 1 10-ounce package frozen peas, thawed
  Freshly grated Parmesan cheese

Brown meat and onion in butter in large kettle over medium heat. Add next 7 ingredients; bring to boil. Reduce heat. Cover; simmer 45 minutes. Stir in rotini. Cook, uncovered, 10 minutes. Stir in peas; cook 3 minutes. Serve with cheese.

Garden Skillet Stew

Makes 4 servings
Preparation Time: 1½ hours

- 1 pound lean beef stew meat
- 2 tablespoons butter
- 1 teaspoon vegetable oil
- 1 cup diced onion
- 2 cups hot beef broth
- 2 teaspoons salt
- ¼ teaspoon ground black pepper
- ½ teaspoon dried dillweed
- ¼ teaspoon dried oregano
- 1 1-pound can stewed tomatoes
- 2 tablespoons tomato paste
- 4 cups sliced green beans
- 4 cups fresh broccoli flowerets
- 1 cup chopped carrots

Brown meat evenly on all sides in butter and oil in skillet over medium-high heat. Add onion during last 5 minutes of browning. Add next 5 ingredients; bring to boil. Cover; simmer 45 minutes. Stir in next 3 ingredients; bring to boil. Cover; simmer 10 minutes. Add broccoli and carrots; bring to boil. Cover; simmer 15 minutes.

30-Minute Skillet Supper

Makes 4 servings
Preparation Time: 30 minutes

- 1 pound Polish sausage, cut in 1-inch diagonal pieces
- 1 medium-size onion, thinly sliced
- 1 16-ounce can sauerkraut, drained
- ½ cup apple juice
- 1 tablespoon light brown sugar, firmly packed
- ¼ teaspoon caraway seed
- ¼ teaspoon salt
- ⅛ teaspoon ground black pepper
- 2 medium-size red cooking apples, sliced

Sauté sausage and onion in skillet over medium heat until onion is translucent. Add sauerkraut; heat through. Stir in next 5 ingredients; bring to boil. Cover; simmer 15 minutes. Add apple slices; cover; simmer 3 minutes.

Yankee Pot Roast

Makes 6 to 8 servings
Preparation Time: 20 minutes; 4 hours to cook

- 3 to 4-pound boneless rolled rump roast *or* boneless chuck blade pot roast
- 2 tablespoons flour
- 1 tablespoon vegetable oil
- 1 medium onion, chopped
- 1 10¾-ounce can condensed onion soup
- ½ cup burgundy wine
- 4 large potatoes, pared and quartered
- 5 carrots, halved
  Few sprigs parsley, chopped

Dredge roast in flour. Heat oil in a large kettle over medium-high heat. Brown roast slowly on all sides. Add next 3 ingredients; cover; simmer 3 hours. Turn once during cooking. Add potatoes, carrots and parsley. Cover; simmer 40 to 50 minutes or until meat and vegetables are tender.

Garden Skillet Stew, this page
Basque-Style Veal Skillet, this page

Leftovers

Chicken Jambalaya Salad

Makes 4 to 6 servings
Preparation Time: 20 minutes; 1 hour to chill

- 4 cups cooked cubed chicken *or* turkey
- 4 cups cooked rice, chilled
- 2 stalks celery, thinly sliced
- 1 cup frozen peas, thawed
- 2 medium-size tomatoes, peeled, seeded, chopped
- 1 medium-size green pepper, chopped
- ½ cup thinly sliced green onion
- ¼ cup minced parsley
- 2 cups plain yogurt
- 2 tablespoons olive oil
- 1 clove garlic, pressed
- 1 tablespoon chili powder
- 1 teaspoon salt
- ¼ teaspoon ground white pepper

Toss first 8 ingredients lightly in large bowl. Beat remaining ingredients in small bowl; pour over chicken. Toss gently; chill 1 hour before serving.

Note: Recipe can be made the night before serving.

Curried Turkey

Makes 4 servings
Preparation Time: 50 minutes

- 2 cups cubed cooked turkey
- ½ cup chopped onion
- ½ cup chopped celery
- ¼ cup chopped green pepper
- 2 tablespoons slivered salted almonds
- 1 4-ounce can button mushrooms, drained
- ½ cup butter *or* margarine
- 1 cup diced tomato
- 2 cups chicken broth
- 1 cup uncooked white rice
- 1 teaspoon curry powder
- 1 teaspoon salt
- ¼ teaspoon ground white pepper
    Fruit chutney
    Raisins
    Kumquats

Sauté first 6 ingredients in butter in 3-quart saucepan over medium heat until lightly browned. Add tomato and broth; bring to boil. Stir in next 4 ingredients; cover; simmer 25 minutes. Let stand 3 to 4 minutes before serving. Serve with fruit chutney, raisins and kumquats as condiments.

Easy Beef Stroganoff

Makes 5 to 6 servings
Preparation Time: 15 minutes

- 4 cups water
- 3 tablespoons butter
- 1 1⅜-ounce package onion soup mix
- ½ pound medium-wide egg noodles
- 2 cups diced cooked beef
- 1 cup dairy sour cream

Bring water, butter and onion soup mix to boil in 12-inch skillet. Stir in noodles; bring to boil; cook 5 minutes. Add beef; cook 4 to 5 more minutes or until noodles are tender. Remove from heat; stir in sour cream. Serve immediately.

Farm-Style Beef Hash

Makes 4 servings
Preparation Time: 15 minutes

- 5 cups frozen hash brown potatoes
- 2 cups diced cooked beef
- 1 medium-size onion, chopped
- ¼ cup butter
- ½ cup beef broth
- ½ teaspoon dried oregano
- ½ teaspoon salt
- ½ teaspoon ground black pepper

Brown potatoes, beef and onion in butter in 10-inch skillet over medium heat 5 minutes. Add remaining ingredients; cover; cook 5 minutes or until potatoes are tender.

Jiffy Turkey Casserole

Makes 5 to 6 servings
Preparation Time: 20 minutes; 1 hour to bake

- 3 cups cooked cubed turkey
- ½ cup chopped celery
- ¼ cup chopped onion
- 1 4-ounce can mushroom stems and pieces, drained
- 1 10¾-ounce can cream of mushroom soup
- ½ cup milk
- 3 cups herb-seasoned croutons

Preheat oven to 350°. Grease 7 by 11-inch baking pan. Cover bottom of pan with turkey. Sprinkle with next 3 ingredients. Blend soup and milk; pour over vegetables. Sprinkle with croutons. Cover; bake 35 minutes.

Rice Potpourri

Makes 4 servings
Preparation Time: 40 minutes

- 1 cup thinly sliced carrot
- ¼ cup margarine
- 2 cups julienne ham strips
- 1 cup sliced green onion
- 3 cups sliced unpeeled apples
- 3 cups cooked rice
- ½ teaspoon salt
- ⅛ teaspoon ground cinnamon
- ½ cup seedless golden raisins
- ¼ cup chopped walnuts

Sauté carrots in margarine in skillet over medium heat 10 minutes. Add ham and onion; cook 3 minutes. Add apples; cook 2 minutes, stirring occasionally. Stir in next 4 ingredients; cook, stirring constantly, until rice is heated. Sprinkle with walnuts before serving.

Tamale Pie

Makes 4 servings
Preparation Time: 20 minutes; 30 minutes to bake

- 2 cups cooked cubed beef or poultry
- 1 12-ounce can whole kernel corn, drained
- ½ cup thinly sliced black olives
- ½ cup finely chopped onion
- 1 clove garlic, pressed
- ⅓ cup chopped green pepper
- 1 8-ounce jar taco sauce
- 1¼ teaspoons salt
- ½ teaspoon dried oregano
- ½ cup grated Cheddar cheese, lightly packed
- ½ cup yellow cornmeal
- ½ cup flour
- 2 teaspoons baking powder
- 1 teaspoon sugar
- 1 egg
- ½ cup milk
- 2 tablespoons margarine or butter

Preheat oven to 400°. Grease 7 by 11-inch baking pan. Mix first 7 ingredients, 1 teaspoon salt and oregano in 2-quart saucepan over medium heat. Bring to boil; simmer 5 minutes. Pour in pan. Sprinkle with cheese. Stir next 4 ingredients and remaining ¼ teaspoon salt in bowl. Add egg, milk and margarine. Beat until smooth, about 1 minute. Spread over cheese; bake 20 to 30 minutes.
Note: Casserole may be prepared ahead to point of making topping and refrigerated. Make topping and bake as directed.

Cauliflower Frenchette

Makes 4 servings
Preparation Time: 45 minutes

- 4 small loaves French bread
- 2 tablespoons butter, melted
- 1 10-ounce package frozen cauliflowerets, thawed
- 2 cups cubed cooked ham
- 1 8-ounce can mushroom stems and pieces, drained
- ⅓ cup sliced green onion
- ¼ cup chopped green pepper
- ½ cup butter
- ⅓ cup flour
- 2½ cups milk
- ⅓ cup dry vermouth wine
- ½ cup shredded Swiss cheese, lightly packed
- ½ teaspoon salt
- ¼ teaspoon ground white pepper
  Dash garlic powder
  Paprika

Preheat oven to 375°. Cut tops off bread. Remove soft center; brush insides with melted butter. Bake about 10 minutes or until hot and crisp. Set aside. Sauté next 5 ingredients in 2 tablespoons butter in 10-inch skillet over medium heat. Remove from heat; cover; keep warm. Melt remaining 6 tablespoons butter in 2-quart saucepan over medium heat. Stir in flour; cook until bubbly. Stir in milk; cook, stirring constantly, until thick and smooth. Stir in wine; boil 1 minute. Remove from heat. Blend in next 4 ingredients, stirring until cheese melts. Stir in ham-vegetable mixture. Heat through over low heat. Use to fill loaves. Sprinkle tops with paprika.

No-Fuss Skillet

Makes 6 servings
Preparation Time: 40 minutes

- 2¼ cups water
- 1 1½-ounce package dry onion soup mix
- 1 cup uncooked rice
  Dash ground black pepper
- 2 cups cooked cubed beef
- 1 10-ounce package frozen peas, thawed
- ¼ cup butter

Bring water and mix to boil in skillet. Stir in rice and pepper; bring to boil. Cover; simmer 10 minutes. Add meat; cover; cook 10 minutes. Stir in peas; cook 5 minutes. Heat butter in small saucepan until brown. Pour over rice, stirring gently. Serve immediately.

Cheddar Crust Meat Pies

Makes 4 servings
Preparation Time: 20 minutes; 30 minutes to bake

- 2 eggs
- 1 10¾-ounce can condensed cream of mushroom soup
- 1 13-ounce can evaporated milk
- 1 cup cooked cubed chicken
- 1 cup cooked cubed ham
- 1 large cooked potato, cut in ⅛-inch thick slices
- 2 cups frozen mixed vegetables, thawed
  Cheddar Crust
  Milk

Preheat oven to 400°. Grease 4 2-cup casserole dishes *or* 1 2-quart shallow baking pan. Beat eggs in bowl. Blend in soup and evaporated milk. Stir in next 4 ingredients; pour into dishes or pan. Roll each Cheddar Crust ball to fit over dishes. Cut slits in top of pastry; brush with milk. Bake 25 to 30 minutes or until crust is golden.

Cheddar Crust

Makes 4

- 1½ cups flour
  Dash salt
- ½ cup shortening
- 1½ cups shredded Cheddar cheese, lightly packed
- 4 to 6 tablespoons ice water

Mix flour and salt in bowl. Cut in shortening using pastry blender until mixture resembles coarse crumbs. Stir in cheese. Sprinkle with water while mixing lightly with fork. Form into 4 balls of dough.

Piraeus Pilaf

Makes 4 to 6 servings
Preparation Time: 30 minutes

- 2¼ cups water
- 1 1½-ounce package onion soup mix
- 3 tablespoons butter
- 1 cup uncooked rice
- 2 cups diced cooked turkey *or* chicken
- ½ cup golden raisins
- ⅓ cup slivered almonds
  Snipped parsley

Bring water, mix and butter to boil in 10-inch skillet. Stir in rice; bring to boil. Cover; simmer 10 minutes. Add next 3 ingredients; bring to boil; cover; simmer 15 minutes. Garnish with parsley.

One-Pot Pasta

Makes 4 to 6 servings
Preparation Time: 30 minutes

- 1 cup chopped onion
- 1 cup chopped celery
- ½ cup chopped green pepper
- ¼ cup butter
- 1 10¾-ounce can condensed cream of celery soup
- 3 cups water
- 1 teaspoon salt
- ½ teaspoon dry mustard
- ⅛ teaspoon ground white pepper
- 4 cups egg noodles
- 1 cup lightly packed shredded Cheddar cheese
- 2 tablespoons grated Parmesan cheese
- 2 cups diced cooked beef
- 1 10-ounce package frozen peas, thawed

Sauté first 3 ingredients in butter in large kettle over medium heat. Add next 5 ingredients; bring to boil. Gradually add noodles so that water continues to boil. Cover; simmer 5 minutes, stirring occasionally. Add next 4 ingredients; cover; cook 2 minutes or until noodles are tender. Toss gently until cheese melts. Serve immediately.

Pasta Bolognese

Makes 4 servings
Preparation Time: 20 minutes

- 2 cups cooked ham, cut in julienne strips
- 1 cup green pepper strips
- ½ cup chopped onion
- 1 clove garlic, pressed
- 3 tablespoons butter
- 3 medium-size tomatoes, diced
- 2 tablespoons dry white wine
- ¼ teaspoon salt
  Dash ground black pepper
- ½ pound linguini *or* spaghetti, cooked, drained
  Grated Parmesan cheese

Sauté first 4 ingredients in butter in large skillet over medium heat 2 to 3 minutes. Add next 4 ingredients; cook 2 to 3 minutes. Pour over linguini *or* spaghetti. Toss; serve with Parmesan cheese.

Cheddar Crust Meat Pies, this page

Leftovers

Meat Medley Salad

Makes 4 to 6 servings
Preparation Time: 30 minutes; 30 minutes to chill

- 4 cups large macaroni shells
- 2 cups plain yogurt
- 1 cup mayonnaise
- 2 tablespoons minced onion
- 2 teaspoons Dijon mustard
- ⅛ teaspoon hot pepper sauce
- ½ teaspoon salt
- ½ teaspoon dried dillweed
- 1 cup cooked cubed beef
- 1 cup cooked cubed ham
- 1 cup cubed salami
- 1 cup diagonally sliced celery
- ⅓ cup sliced pimiento-stuffed olives
- 1 to 1½-quarts assorted salad greens

Cook macaroni shells according to package directions; drain; rinse with cold water; drain again; chill. Mix next 7 ingredients in large bowl. Add next 5 ingredients and macaroni. Toss to coat meat and vegetables. Arrange half of salad greens in large glass bowl. Top with half of macaroni mixture. Top with remaining salad greens and macaroni mixture. Chill 30 minutes.

Beef Tabbouleh

Makes 4 servings
Preparation Time: 30 minutes; 1 hour to chill

- 1 cup bulgur or cracked wheat
- 3 cups hot water
- 1½ cups cooked cubed beef
- 1 cup minced celery
- ½ cup thinly sliced green onion
- ½ cup minced parsley
- 1 cup plain yogurt
- ¼ cup olive oil
- 2 teaspoons white wine vinegar
- 1¼ teaspoons salt
- 1 small clove garlic, pressed
  Lemon wedges

Put bulgur in medium-size bowl; pour in hot water; let stand 30 minutes. Drain; place bulgur in large bowl. Add next 4 ingredients; toss. Stir yogurt in small bowl until creamy. Drizzle in next 4 ingredients; pour over bulgur. Toss; cover; chill 1 hour. Garnish with lemon wedges before serving.

Variation: Three cups cooked white rice can be substituted for bulgur. Omit soaking rice in hot water.

Turkey Tetrazzini

Makes 6 servings
Preparation Time: 40 minutes; 20 minutes to bake

- ½ pound spaghetti, broken in half
- ½ pound sliced mushrooms
- ½ cup chopped onion
- ¼ cup butter
- 2 tablespoons flour
- 2½ cups milk or half-and-half
- ¼ cup dry white wine
- ½ teaspoon salt
- ¼ teaspoon ground white pepper
- 2 tablespoons diced pimiento, drained
- 2 cups cooked cubed turkey
- 2 cups broccoli flowerets, cooked
- 1½ cups shredded brick or Muenster cheese, lightly packed

Preheat oven to 400°. Grease 9 by 13-inch baking pan. Cook spaghetti according to package directions; drain. Arrange in pan, leaving well in center. Sauté mushrooms and onion in butter in large saucepan. Add flour; cook, stirring 1 to 2 minutes. Add next 4 ingredients; cook, stirring, until slightly thickened. Fold in pimiento. Remove 1 cup sauce; pour over spaghetti in pan. Add turkey and broccoli to remaining sauce. Spoon into well in pan. Sprinkle with cheese; cover; bake 20 minutes.

Ham Supreme

Makes 4 to 6 servings
Preparation Time: 10 minutes; 30 minutes to bake

- 2 cups medium-size egg noodles, cooked and drained
- 1 16-ounce can French-style green beans, drained
- 1½ cups diced cooked ham
- 1 10¾-ounce can condensed cream of celery soup
- 1¼ cups milk
- ¾ cup grated Cheddar cheese, lightly packed
- 2 tablespoons minced parsley
- 2 tablespoons chopped pimiento, drained
- 1 tablespoon instant minced onion
- ½ can French-fried onion rings

Preheat oven to 375°. Grease 9-inch square baking pan. Put noodles in pan. Top with beans and ham. Mix next 6 ingredients in bowl. Pour in pan; top evenly with onion rings. Bake 25 to 30 minutes.

Tarragon Stuffed Peppers

Makes 4 servings
Preparation Time: 45 minutes; 1 hour to bake

- 1 pound lean ground beef
- 1 cup chopped onion
- 1 clove minced garlic
- 2 cups chopped celery
- 1½ cups chopped zucchini
- 1 cup sliced mushrooms
- ½ cup chopped carrot
- ¼ cup chopped parsley
- 1¼ cups tomato juice
- ½ teaspoon dried tarragon
- ½ teaspoon salt
- ¼ teaspoon ground black pepper
- 4 large green peppers, halved lengthwise, seeds and membranes removed

Preheat oven to 400°. Brown ground beef, onion and garlic in 10-inch skillet, stirring to break up meat. Drain off fat; stir in next 5 ingredients, ¼ cup tomato juice, tarragon, salt and pepper. Cook 3 minutes. Stuff each pepper half with mixture, pressing and mounding high. Arrange in 9 by 13-inch baking pan. Pour remaining 1 cup tomato juice in pan. Cover; bake 20 minutes. Reduce heat to 350°; bake 20 minutes. Uncover; bake 15 minutes or until peppers are tender. Contains about 329 calories per serving.

Tasty Tuna Salad

Makes 2 servings
Preparation Time: 10 minutes

- 1 7-ounce can water-packed tuna, drained
- 1½ cups chopped celery
- ½ cup shredded carrot
- ½ cup chopped onion
- 2 ounces crumbled feta cheese
- 2 tablespoons lemon juice
- 1 tablespoon mayonnaise-style salad dressing
- ⅛ teaspoon dried dillweed
- ⅛ teaspoon ground white pepper
- ⅛ teaspoon garlic powder

Flake tuna in medium-size bowl. Add next 4 ingredients; toss. Mix next 5 ingredients; pour over tuna; toss. Cover; chill 30 minutes before serving, if desired. Contains about 275 calories per serving.

Chicken Ratatouille

Makes 4 servings
Preparation Time: 30 minutes; 1 hour to bake

- 2 cups diagonally sliced celery
- 1 cup sliced zucchini
- 1 cup thinly sliced carrots
- 1 medium-size onion, cut in rings
- 1 cup sliced mushrooms
- ¼ cup uncooked rice
- 1 cup tomato juice
- ½ cup chicken broth
- 1 clove garlic, pressed
- 1 2½-pound broiler-fryer chicken, cut in serving pieces
- 1½ teaspoons salt
- ¼ teaspoon paprika
- ⅛ teaspoon ground black pepper

Preheat oven to 375°. Arrange first 5 ingredients in bottom of 9 by 13-inch baking pan. Sprinkle with rice. Bring tomato juice, broth and garlic to boil in saucepan; pour over vegetables. Rub chicken with salt, paprika and pepper. Place skin-side-up, over vegetables. Cover; bake 1 hour. Uncover; bake 20 minutes or until chicken is tender. Contains 223 calories per serving.

Savory Cube Steaks

Makes 2 servings
Preparation Time: 40 minutes

- 1 teaspoon butter
- 2 beef cube steaks
- ½ teaspoon salt
- ½ teaspoon dried oregano
- ¼ teaspoon garlic powder
- ⅛ teaspoon ground black pepper
- 2 cups broccoli flowerets
- 1 medium-size onion, peeled, sliced
- ½ cup chopped celery
- ½ cup thin green pepper strips
- 1 8-ounce can tomato sauce
- ¼ cup shredded carrot, optional

Brush 10-inch skillet with butter. Sprinkle cube steaks with next 4 ingredients. Brown each side 7 minutes over medium heat. Remove; set aside. Sauté next 5 ingredients 10 minutes. Top with steaks; cook 5 minutes. Sprinkle with shredded carrot, if desired, before serving. Contains about 512 calories per serving.

Hong Kong Stir-Fry

Makes 4 servings
Preparation Time: 30 minutes

- 1 tablespoon oil
- 1 cup sliced mushrooms
- 2 green peppers, cored, cut in julienne strips
- 1 medium-size onion, peeled, cut in thin strips
- 1 clove garlic, minced
- 2 cups cooked julienne strips of beef
- 1 6-ounce package frozen pea pods
- ¼ cup soy sauce
- ¼ cup beef broth
- 2 cups hot cooked rice

Heat oil in wok *or* 10-inch skillet over medium-high heat. Add first 4 ingredients; cook, stirring 2 minutes. Add next 4 ingredients; cook, stirring 3 minutes. Serve over hot cooked rice. Contains about 352 calories per serving.

Vegetable Chicken Chop Suey

Makes 4 servings
Preparation Time: 20 minutes; 15 minutes to cook

- ½ cup uncooked rice
- 2 whole chicken breasts, skinned, boned, split, cut in julienne strips
- 1½ cups chicken broth
- 1 teaspoon sesame oil
- 4 cups diagonally sliced celery
- ½ pound Chinese cabbage, cut in thin slices
- 1 8-ounce can sliced bamboo shoots, drained
- 1 cup sliced mushrooms
- 1 cup bean sprouts
- 1 6-ounce package frozen pea pods, thawed
- 1 red *or* green pepper, cored, cut in thin strips
- 1 small onion, peeled, cut in thin slices
- ¼ cup soy sauce
- 1 slice fresh gingerroot, finely chopped
- 1 tablespoon cornstarch

Cook rice according to package directions; set aside; keep hot. Cook chicken and ¼ cup chicken broth in wok or large skillet over medium-high heat 4 to 5 minutes. Add sesame oil, celery and 1 cup chicken broth; bring to boil. Reduce heat; cook 5 minutes. Add next 9 ingredients. Dissolve cornstarch in ¼ cup cold chicken broth; stir into vegetable mixture. Bring to boil; cook 5 minutes or until vegetables are heated through. Serve over hot cooked rice. Contains about 310 calories per serving.

Continental Chicken

Makes 2 servings
Preparation Time: 30 minutes; 35 minutes to bake

- ½ teaspoon salt
- ¼ teaspoon ground black pepper
- ¼ teaspoon paprika
- ¼ teaspoon garlic powder
- ¼ teaspoon celery seed
- ¼ teaspoon dried dillweed
- 2 whole chicken breasts, skinned, split
- 1 teaspoon butter
- 2 cups cauliflowerets
- ½ pound sliced green beans
- 1 8-ounce can mushroom stems and pieces, drained
- 1 cup sliced carrot
- ½ cup tomato juice
- 3 tablespoons instant chopped onion

Preheat oven to 375°. Mix first 6 ingredients; rub over chicken pieces. Brush 10-inch skillet with butter. Heat. Add chicken, browning lightly on each side. Remove from heat; set aside. Place next 4 ingredients in 7 by 11-inch baking pan. Mix tomato juice with onion; pour over vegetables. Arrange chicken over vegetables. Cover; bake 30 to 35 minutes. Contains about 400 calories per serving.

Fish Fiesta

Makes 4 servings
Preparation Time: 45 minutes

- 1 medium-size onion, peeled, thinly sliced
- 1½ pounds fresh *or* frozen cod *or* haddock fillets, thawed
- 1 tablespoon lemon juice
- ½ teaspoon salt
- ¼ teaspoon dried dillweed
- ⅛ teaspoon ground white pepper
- 2 green peppers, cored, quartered
- 2 medium-size tomatoes, chopped
- 1 6-ounce package frozen pea pods
- ½ cup dry white wine
- 2 tablespoons minced parsley
  Lemon wedges

Preheat oven to 350°. Spray 7 by 11-inch baking pan with vegetable cooking spray. Spread onion over bottom of pan. Top with fish. Sprinkle with next 4 ingredients. Arrange green peppers, tomatoes and pea pods over fish. Top with wine. Bake for 25 to 30 minutes or until fish flakes easily when tested with fork. Sprinkle with parsley; serve with lemon wedges. Contains about 331 calories per serving.

Low Calorie

Turkey Fruit Salad

Makes 2 servings
Preparation Time: 30 minutes

- 6 ounces diced cooked turkey *or* chicken
  Dash salt
  Dash ground white pepper
- ½ cup chopped celery
- 1 medium-size apple, cored, diced
- 1 medium-size pear, cored, diced
- 1 small banana, peeled, sliced
- ½ cup plain yogurt
- 1 teaspoon sugar
- 1 small cantaloupe

Sprinkle turkey with salt and pepper in bowl. Add next 4 ingredients. Mix yogurt and sugar; pour over turkey mixture; toss well. Halve cantaloupe lengthwise; remove seeds. Cut thin slice from bottom of each half so it will stand on plate. Spoon ½ turkey mixture into each cantaloupe half. Serve immediately. Contains about 429 calories per serving.

Veal Italiano

Makes 4 servings
Preparation time: 20 minutes; 1 hour to cook

- 1 pound lean veal, cut in 1-inch cubes
- ½ cup chopped onion
- 2 cloves garlic, minced
- 1 tablespoon butter
- 2 cups sliced green beans
- 2 cups tomato juice
- 1 teaspoon dried dillweed
- 1 teaspoon salt
- ¼ teaspoon ground white pepper
- 2 cups diagonally sliced celery
- 1 cup sliced carrot
- 2 small zucchini, sliced

Brown veal, onion and garlic in butter in large kettle over medium heat. Add next 5 ingredients; bring to boil. Cover; simmer 40 minutes. Add celery, carrots and zucchini; bring to boil. Cover; simmer 20 minutes. Contains about 369 calories per serving.

Shrimp Creole

Makes 2 servings
Preparation Time: 20 minutes; 30 minutes to cook

- 1 cup tomato juice *or* 2 medium-size tomatoes, coarsely chopped
- ½ cup water
- ¼ cup uncooked rice
- 1½ cups chopped celery with leaves
- ½ cup chopped onion
- ½ cup chopped green pepper
- 2 cloves garlic, pressed
- 1 teaspoon parsley flakes
- ½ teaspoon paprika
- ¼ teaspoon salt
- ⅛ teaspoon cayenne pepper
- 1 bay leaf
- 7 ounces fresh *or* frozen shrimp, thawed

Bring tomato juice and water to boil in 10-inch skillet. Add next 10 ingredients; bring to boil. Cover; simmer 15 minutes. Stir in shrimp; cover; simmer 10 minutes. Contains about 260 calories per serving.

Skillet Supper

Makes 2 servings
Preparation Time: 25 minutes

- 14 ounces lean ground beef
- 2 cups diagonally sliced celery
- 1 cup chopped onion
- ½ cup tomato juice
- ¼ cup minced parsley
- ½ teaspoon dried dillweed
- ½ teaspoon salt
- ⅛ teaspoon ground black pepper
- 1 15½-ounce can French-style green beans, drained
- 1 4-ounce can mushroom stems and pieces, drained

Brown meat in 10-inch skillet over medium heat; drain off fat. Add celery and onion; sauté 2 to 3 minutes. Stir in next 5 ingredients; bring to boil. Reduce heat; cover; simmer 10 minutes. Add beans and mushrooms; bring to boil. Reduce heat; cover; cook 5 minutes to heat beans. Contains about 511 calories per serving.

Fish & Seafood

Baked Fillet Swirls

Makes 4 servings
Preparation Time: 20 minutes; 20 minutes to bake

- 8 pike fish fillets (thawed if frozen)
- 1 tablespoon lemon juice
- 2 cups zucchini slices, cut in quarters
- 3 cups chopped tomato
- 1 cup chopped onion
- 1 cup chopped green pepper
- ¼ cup butter
- ½ cup minced parsley
- 1 teaspoon dried dill weed
- 1 teaspoon salt
- 1 teaspoon paprika
- ⅓ cup dry white wine
- 2 slices processed American cheese, cut in thin strips

Preheat oven to 400°. Sprinkle fish with lemon juice; set aside. Sauté next 7 ingredients and ½ teaspoon salt in 10-inch skillet. Cook 3 minutes. Sprinkle fish with remaining ½ teaspoon salt and paprika. Roll skin-side-inside and place in 9-inch square baking pan. Fill centers of fish rolls with vegetable mixture. Pour wine in pan. Bake 15 minutes or until fish flakes easily. Top with cheese strips. Bake 5 minutes.

Salmon Casserole

Makes 4 to 6 servings
Preparation Time: 20 minutes; 20 minutes to bake

- 1 10-ounce package frozen mixed vegetables, thawed
- 1 cup plain yogurt
- 1 10¾-ounce can condensed cream of celery soup
- 1 15½-ounce can salmon, drained, skin and bones removed
- 2 cups cooked rice
- ½ cup chopped onion
- 1 teaspoon dried dillweed
- ⅛ teaspoon ground white pepper
- ½ cup crushed cornflake crumbs
- 4 pitted ripe olives, sliced
  Parsley sprigs

Preheat oven to 350°. Grease 2-quart casserole dish. Blend together yogurt and soup in large bowl. Stir in next 6 ingredients; pour into dish; top with cornflake crumbs. Cover; bake 20 minutes. Garnish with sliced olives and parsley sprigs.

Crab Soufflé

Makes 4 servings
Preparation Time: 35 minutes; 40 minutes to bake

- ¼ cup butter
- ¼ cup flour
- 1 cup cold milk or half-and-half
- 1 teaspoon dried dillweed
- ½ teaspoon salt
- ⅛ teaspoon paprika
- ⅛ teaspoon cayenne pepper
- 4 jumbo eggs, separated, at room temperature
- 1 6-ounce package frozen crab meat, thawed, drained, flaked
- ½ cup shredded Swiss cheese, lightly packed
- ⅛ teaspoon cream of tartar

Preheat oven to 350°. Grease 6-cup soufflé dish. Melt ¼ cup butter in 2-quart saucepan. Stir in flour; cook, stirring until bubbly. Do not brown flour. Stir in next 5 ingredients; cook, stirring until thickened. Remove from heat. Beat yolks. Stir ½ cup hot sauce into yolks. Stir in crab meat and cheese. (Soufflé can be prepared several hours in advance to this point.) If sauce was made ahead, heat over low heat to luke-warm. Beat whites with cream of tartar until stiff, but not dry. Whisk about 1 cup whites into sauce. Fold in remaining whites with rubber spatula. Pour into dish; bake 40 minutes. Serve immediately.

Creamy Crab Quiche

Makes 4 to 5 servings
Preparation Time: 20 minutes; 40 minutes to bake

- 4 eggs
- 1 13-ounce can evaporated milk
- ½ teaspoon salt
- ½ teaspoon dry mustard
  Dash cayenne pepper
- 1 6-ounce package frozen crab meat, thawed, drained, flaked
- 1 cup shredded Swiss cheese, lightly packed
- ⅓ cup thinly sliced green onions
- 1 9-inch baked pie crust
  Paprika

Preheat oven to 375°. Beat first 5 ingredients in bowl; stir in crab, cheese and onion. Pour into crust; sprinkle with paprika. Bake 35 to 40 minutes. Let stand 5 minutes before cutting.

Fish & Seafood

Captain's Crab Meat

Makes 6 servings
Preparation Time: 40 minutes

- ¼ cup butter
- ½ pound mushrooms, thinly sliced
- 1 small green pepper, cored, cut in julienne strips
- ½ cup diced celery
- ½ cup thinly sliced green onion
- 2 10¾-ounce cans condensed cream of celery soup
- ¼ cup fresh lemon juice
- ¼ cup chopped pimiento, drained
- ¼ cup sliced black olives
- 2 tablespoons minced parsley
- ½ teaspoon celery salt
- ¼ teaspoon salt
- ⅛ teaspoon hot pepper sauce
- 2 6-ounce packages frozen crab meat, thawed, drained, flaked or 2 6-ounce cans drained, cartilage removed, flaked
- 4 cups cooked white rice or 6 frozen patty shells, baked according to package directions
- ½ cup slivered almonds, toasted

Melt butter in large skillet. Add next 4 ingredients; cook, stirring until vegetables are tender, about 5 minutes. Stir in next 8 ingredients; heat until hot. Stir in crab meat; heat through. Serve over rice or in patty shells. Sprinkle with almonds.

Cheese-Topped Tuna

Makes 4 servings
Preparation Time: 20 minutes; 30 minutes to bake

- 1 1-pound can sliced potatoes, drained
- ⅓ cup water
- ⅓ cup dry white wine
- 2 hard-cooked eggs
  Few drops hot pepper sauce
- 1 cup chopped onion
- 1 cup chopped celery
- 1 clove garlic, minced
- 2 tablespoons olive oil
- 2 7-ounce cans tuna, drained
- ¼ cup pimiento-stuffed olives
- ½ cup mayonnaise
- 2 tablespoons lemon juice
- 1 teaspoon horseradish
- 1 tablespoon chopped parsley
- ½ cup shredded Cheddar cheese, lightly packed
- ¼ cup chopped almonds

Preheat oven to 350°. Grease 9-inch baking pan. Place first 5 ingredients in food processor container or blender. Process 1 minute until smooth. Sauté next 3 ingredients in oil in skillet until onion is translucent. Break tuna into chunks in bowl. Add potato mixture, onion mixture and next 5 ingredients. Spoon into pan; bake 20 minutes. Cover with cheese; sprinkle with almonds. Bake 10 minutes, or until cheese melts.

Fish Stew Marinara

Makes 4 servings
Preparation Time: 30 minutes; 1 hour to cook

- 2 tablespoons olive oil
- 2 medium-size onions, chopped
- 1 clove garlic, minced
- 2 tablespoons minced parsley
- 1 cup water
- ½ teaspoon salt
- ½ teaspoon dried oregano
- ½ teaspoon dried marjoram
- 1 bay leaf
  Marinara sauce
- 2 carrots, cut in 1-inch coins
- 2 potatoes, pared, cubed
- ½ cup diced celery
- 2 pounds firm white fish fillets (halibut, haddock or cod) thawed, if frozen, cut in pieces
- 1 lemon, thinly sliced
- 1 6½-ounce can chopped clams, drained

Heat oil in large kettle over medium heat. Sauté onion and garlic until onion is translucent. Add next 6 ingredients and Marinara sauce; simmer 10 minutes. Stir in carrots, potatoes and celery; bring to boil; reduce heat; cook 10 minutes. Add fish and lemon slices; simmer 10 minutes or until fish flakes easily. Stir in clams and heat through.

Marinara Sauce

- 1 medium-size onion, chopped
- 3 tablespoons olive oil
- 1 1-pound can tomatoes with juice, chopped
- 1 8-ounce can tomato sauce
- 1 teaspoon granulated sugar
- ½ teaspoon salt
- ½ teaspoon dried oregano
- ½ teaspoon dried thyme
- ¼ teaspoon ground black pepper

Sauté onion in oil in 2-quart saucepan until onion is translucent. Stir in remaining ingredients; bring to boil. Reduce heat; cover; simmer 30 minutes.

Captain's Crab Meat, this page

Fish & Seafood

Salmon Rarebit

Makes 4 servings
Preparation Time: 15 minutes

- 1 tablespoon butter
- 1 tablespoon flour
- 1 cup milk
- ½ cup tomato puree
- 1 tablespoon Worcestershire sauce
- 1 teaspoon mustard
- ½ teaspoon salt
- 2 eggs, lightly beaten
- 1 cup shredded Cheddar cheese, lightly packed
- 1 15½-ounce can salmon, boned, broken in large pieces
- 4 slices bread, toasted
- ¼ cup thinly sliced green onion

Melt butter in 2-quart saucepan. Add flour; cook, stirring until bubbly. Add milk; cook, stirring constantly, until slightly thickened. Stir in next 4 ingredients; cook, stirring constantly, until bubbly. Add about 2 tablespoons hot sauce to beaten eggs in bowl. Stir egg mixture into sauce slowly. Cook 1 minute. Stir in cheese until melted. Stir in salmon; heat through. Serve immediately over toast. Sprinkle with green onion.

Shrimp Foo Yung

Makes 4 servings
Preparation Time: 15 minutes

- 1 cup diced shrimp *or* 1 cup diced cooked chicken
- ¼ cup minced green onion
- ¼ cup minced celery
- ½ cup drained mixed Chinese vegetables
- ½ teaspoon salt
- 4 eggs
- 2 tablespoons vegetable oil
  Oriental sauce

Mix first 5 ingredients in bowl. Beat eggs in bowl; add to shrimp mixture. Heat oil in 12-inch skillet over medium heat. Divide mixture into 4 portions; place in pan; brown several minutes on each side. Place on heated platter; serve with Oriental Sauce.

Oriental Sauce

- 1 tablespoon granulated sugar
- 1 tablespoon cornstarch
- ⅛ teaspoon dry mustard
- 2 tablespoons soy sauce
- 1¼ cups chicken broth

Mix first 3 ingredients in 1-quart saucepan. Blend in soy sauce and chicken broth. Cook, stirring constantly, until sauce bubbles and thickens, 2 to 3 minutes.

Tuna Scallop

Makes 4 servings
Preparation Time: 15 minutes; 45 minutes to bake

- 5 slices white bread, crusts removed, cubed
- 1 7-ounce can chunk light tuna, drained, flaked
- ½ cup pimiento-stuffed olives, halved
- 1½ cups shredded Cheddar cheese, lightly packed
- 3 eggs
- 1 cup milk
- ¼ cup dry white wine
- 1 tablespoon instant chopped onion
- 1 teaspoon Worcestershire sauce
- ¾ teaspoon salt
- ¼ teaspoon ground white pepper

Preheat oven to 350°. Grease 1½-quart baking dish. Place bread cubes in dish; top with tuna and olives. Cover with cheese. Beat eggs in bowl. Stir in next 6 ingredients; pour over casserole. Bake 45 minutes or until set in center.

Cioppino

Makes 6 servings
Preparation Time: 15 minutes; 27 minutes to cook

- 1½ pounds assorted fish fillets (thawed if frozen)
- 1 tablespoon lemon juice
- 2 potatoes, pared, diced
- 1 cup chopped onion
- ¼ cup chopped celery
- ¼ cup chopped green pepper
- ¼ cup chopped parsley
- 1 clove garlic, pressed
- ⅓ cup olive oil
- 1 16-ounce can tomatoes with juice
- 1 8-ounce can tomato sauce
- 1 cup dry red wine
- 1 teaspoon salt
- ½ teaspoon dried oregano
- ¼ teaspoon ground white pepper
- 1 cup chopped zucchini
- 2 6½-ounce cans whole clams, drained

Sprinkle fillets with lemon juice; let stand. Sauté next 6 ingredients in oil in large kettle until onion is translucent. Add next 6 ingredients; bring to boil. Boil 5 minutes. Cut fillets in 1-inch pieces; add to kettle with zucchini. Bring to boil. Reduce heat; simmer 20 minutes or until fish flakes easily. Add clams and heat through, about 2 minutes. Serve immediately.

Hot Taco Salad

Makes 4 servings
Preparation Time: 20 minutes

- 1 pound lean ground beef
- ½ cup minced onion
- 3 medium-size tomatoes, cubed
- 1 8-ounce jar taco sauce
- 2 teaspoons paprika
- 1 teaspoon cumin
- ½ teaspoon salt
- ½ teaspoon garlic salt
- ¼ teaspoon hot pepper sauce
- 1 medium-size head lettuce, shredded
- 1 15-ounce can kidney beans, drained
- 1 cup shredded Cheddar cheese, lightly packed
- ½ cup thinly sliced green onion
  Corn chips

Brown beef and onion in 10-inch skillet over medium heat, stirring to break up meat. Add next 7 ingredients; cook 5 minutes. Divide lettuce into four portions; place on dinner plates. Top each with ¼ of beans. Spoon ¼ of beef mixture over beans. Sprinkle with cheese and onion. Garnish with corn chips.

Veal Scallopini

Makes 4 servings
Preparation Time: 15 minutes; 30 minutes to bake

- 4 veal steaks (about 1½ pounds)
- ⅓ cup butter
- 1 medium-size onion, thinly sliced
- 1 cup uncooked rice
- 1 8-ounce can tomato sauce
- 1 cup chicken broth
- ¼ cup dry white wine
- 1 clove garlic, pressed
- 1 tablespoon lemon juice
- 1 teaspoon salt
- ⅛ teaspoon ground white pepper
- 1 green pepper, cored, cut in rings
- 1 4-ounce can button mushrooms, drained
- 8 pimiento-stuffed olives

Preheat oven to 375°. Brown veal on both sides in butter in large skillet over medium heat. Remove veal. Sauté onion and rice in drippings until onion is translucent. Add next 7 ingredients; bring to boil. Pour in 9 by 13-inch baking pan; cover; bake 15 minutes. Uncover; arrange veal, pepper rings, mushrooms and olives over rice. Cover; bake 15 minutes. Let stand 5 minutes before serving.

Mexicali Corn Pie

Makes 4 servings
Preparation Time: 30 minutes; 30 minutes to bake

- 1 cup instant potato flakes
- ½ cup flour
- ¼ cup grated Parmesan cheese
- ⅛ teaspoon salt
- ⅓ cup butter
- ¼ cup milk
- 1 pound lean ground beef
- 1 medium-size onion, thinly sliced
- 1 12-ounce can whole kernel corn, drained
- 2 green chilies, chopped
- 2 tablespoons tomato paste
- ½ teaspoon salt
- 1 cup shredded Cheddar cheese, lightly packed

Preheat oven to 350°. Combine first 4 ingredients; cut in butter to resemble coarse crumbs. Stir in milk until dough holds together. Press into bottom and sides of 9-inch pie pan. Prick in several places using fork. Bake 20 minutes. Cool. Brown beef and onion in large skillet, stirring to break up meat. Stir in next 5 ingredients; spread in crust. Sprinkle cheese over top; bake 10 minutes. Serve immediately.

Hungarian Goulash

Makes 6 servings
Preparation Time: 20 minutes; 1½ hours to cook

- 1 tablespoon vegetable oil
- 2 pounds lean boneless pork, cut in 1-inch cubes
- 2 large onions, chopped
- 1 clove garlic, minced
- 1 cup water
- ⅓ cup dry white wine
- 1 tablespoon paprika
- 1 teaspoon caraway seed
- 1 teaspoon salt
- ⅛ teaspoon ground black pepper
- 1 27-ounce can sauerkraut, drained
- 1 cup dairy sour cream
  Chopped parsley

Heat oil in large kettle over medium heat. Brown pork on all sides. Add onions and garlic; sauté until onions are translucent. Drain off fat; add next 6 ingredients. Bring to a boil; reduce heat. Cover; simmer 1 hour. Add sauerkraut; heat to boiling; reduce heat. Cover; simmer 30 minutes. Remove from heat; stir in sour cream and sprinkle with parsley.

International

Salonika Lamb in Foil

Makes 6 servings
Preparation Time: 30 minutes; chill 4 hours or overnight; bake 2 hours

    Juice of 1 lemon
3 tablespoons olive oil
1 clove garlic, pressed
1 tablespoon dried oregano
1 tablespoon salt
1 teaspoon ground black pepper
3 pounds leg of lamb, fat trimmed, cut into ½-pound servings
6 small potatoes, pared
6 small carrots, halved
6 small onions
12 celery stalks, cut in 3-inch pieces
18 ripe Greek olives
½ pound feta cheese, cut in 6 pieces

Preheat oven to 375°. Beat first 6 ingredients in bowl; pour over lamb in pan. Marinate 4 hours or overnight in refrigerator. Cut 6 squares of heavy-duty foil large enough to hold one serving. Place 1 serving lamb in center of foil. Add 1 potato, 1 carrot, 1 onion, 2 pieces celery and 3 olives. Top with cheese. Repeat with remaining portions. Wrap securely; place in baking pan. Bake 2 hours or until meat is done.

Paella

Makes 6 servings
Preparation Time: 1 hour

1 3-pound broiler-fryer chicken, cut in serving pieces
1 teaspoon salt
½ teaspoon ground black pepper
¼ cup olive oil
1 large onion, chopped
1 cup chopped tomato or 1 1-pound can tomatoes, chopped, drained
1 clove garlic, minced
2 cups chicken broth
2 tablespoons minced parsley
¼ cup diced pimiento, drained
¼ teaspoon powdered saffron or ground turmeric
1 cup uncooked rice
1 cup shelled, deveined raw shrimp or frozen shrimp, thawed
1 cup frozen peas, thawed
4 artichoke hearts, halved
6 mussels or clams, optional
    Pimiento strips
    Parsley sprigs

Sprinkle chicken with ½ teaspoon salt and ¼ teaspoon pepper. Brown in hot oil in large kettle over medium heat about 10 minutes. Re- move chicken; set aside. Sauté onion, tomato and garlic in drippings until onion is translucent. Add next 4 ingredients, remaining ½ teaspoon salt and ¼ teaspoon pepper. Bring to boil; stir in rice. Bring to boil; cover; simmer 10 minutes. Add chicken; cover; cook 15 minutes. Add shrimp, peas and artichoke hearts; cover; cook 5 minutes or until shrimp is tender. Steam mussels or clams in a little boiling water in large kettle until shells open. Use to garnish Paella along with pimiento strips and parsley sprigs. Serve immediately.

Chicken Provençale

Makes 4 servings
Preparation Time: 20 minutes; 1¼ hours to cook

4 whole chicken breasts, split
2 tablespoons lemon juice
1 teaspoon salt
½ teaspoon dried oregano
⅛ teaspoon ground white pepper
2 tablespoons olive oil
1 tablespoon butter
    Herb Sauce
12 ounces thin spaghetti, broken in half
    Grated Parmesan cheese

Sprinkle chicken with lemon juice, salt, oregano and pepper. Heat oil and butter in large skillet on medium heat. Add chicken breasts skin-side-down; cover; cook 10 minutes. Turn; cover; cook 5 minutes. Add hot Herb Sauce; cover; simmer 30 minutes. Stir once during cooking. Cook spaghetti according to package directions; drain. Place on large warm platter. Arrange chicken on spaghetti; top with sauce. Serve with cheese.

Herb Sauce

1 15-ounce can tomato sauce
¾ cup water
2 tablespoons tomato paste
1 large clove garlic, pressed
1 tablespoon minced parsley
1½ teaspoons dried oregano
1 teaspoon salt
¾ teaspoon dried basil
½ teaspoon granulated sugar
¼ teaspoon ground black pepper

Mix all ingredients in saucepan. Bring to a boil; set aside.

International

Beef Enchiladas

Makes 4 servings
Preparation Time: 45 minutes; 30 minutes to bake

- 1 pound lean ground beef
- 1 cup thinly sliced green onion
- 1 clove garlic, minced
- 1 8-ounce can tomato sauce
- 1 8-ounce can stewed tomatoes
- 1 green chili pepper, chopped
- 1½ teaspoons chili powder
- ½ teaspoon salt
- ½ cup dairy sour cream
  Vegetable oil
- 8 corn tortillas
- 2 cups shredded Cheddar cheese, lightly packed
- 2 cups shredded lettuce
  Sliced black olives

Preheat oven to 400°. Lightly grease 9 by 13-inch baking pan. Brown beef in large skillet, stirring to break up meat. Add onion and garlic during last few minutes of browning. Stir in next 5 ingredients; simmer 5 to 7 minutes. Remove from heat; cool slightly. Stir in sour cream. Heat 1 teaspoon oil in an 8-inch skillet. Sauté one tortilla lightly on each side. (Tortillas should *not* be crisp). Drain on paper towel. Repeat with remaining tortillas using more oil if needed. Spoon about ½ cup filling down center of each tortilla. Roll; place in pan. Cover with foil; bake 15 minutes. Uncover; sprinkle with Cheddar cheese. Cover with foil; bake 3 minutes or until cheese melts. Serve over shredded lettuce, garnished with black olives.

Beef Steefatho

Makes 6 servings
Preparation Time: 40 minutes; 2¼ hours to cook

- ¼ cup olive oil
- 2 pounds lean beef chuck, cut in 1½-inch cubes
- 2 cloves garlic, pressed
- 1½ tablespoons mixed pickling spice
- 1½ cups hot water
- 3 pounds small white onions, peeled
- 1 8-ounce can tomato sauce
- 3 tablespoons tomato paste
- ½ cup vinegar
- 1 tablespoon salt
- ¼ teaspoon ground black pepper

Heat oil in a large kettle over medium heat. Brown meat evenly on all sides. Add garlic during last few minutes of browning. Tie pickling spice in cheesecloth; place in kettle. Add water; cover; simmer 1¼ hours. Add onions. Mix remaining ingredients; pour over meat and onions. Liquid should half cover contents in kettle; if not, add more hot water. Place heavy heatproof plate upside-down in kettle over meat and onions to keep onions intact during cooking. Bring to boil; cover; simmer 45 minutes. Remove plate and spice bag before serving.

Deep-Dish Pizza

Makes 4 to 6 servings
Preparation Time: 40 minutes; 35 minutes to bake

- ¼ cup chopped onion
- 2 cloves garlic, pressed
- 2 tablespoons butter
- ½ pound mushrooms, sliced
- 1 teaspoon dried oregano
- ½ teaspoon salt
  Dash ground black pepper
- 1 4-ounce can stewed tomatoes
- ¼ cup tomato paste
- ¼ cup grated Parmesan cheese
- 3 tablespoons water
  Pizza Dough
- ½ cup sliced pepperoni
- 1 medium-size onion, cut in rings
- 1 small green pepper, cored, cut in thin strips
- 4 cups shredded mozzarella cheese, lightly packed

Preheat oven to 425°. Sauté onion and garlic in butter in skillet over medium heat. Add next 4 ingredients; cook 2 to 3 minutes. Add next 4 ingredients; bring to boil. Simmer 1 minute; set aside. Grease 2-inch deep 12-inch round pizza pan. Press Pizza Dough evenly in pan and halfway up sides. Cover; let dough rise 20 to 30 minutes. Bake 20 minutes. Spoon sauce over dough. Top with pepperoni, onion rings and green pepper strips. Bake 7 minutes. Sprinkle with cheese; bake 3 to 5 minutes. Let stand 2 to 3 minutes before serving.

Pizza Dough

- 1 package active dry yeast
- 1 cup warm water (105° to 115°F)
- 1 teaspoon granulated sugar
- ½ teaspoon salt
- 3 tablespoons vegetable oil
- 2½ cups flour

Sprinkle yeast on warm water in large bowl. Stir in remaining ingredients; beat with wooden spoon or knead by hand 1 minute. Let rest 10 minutes.

Arroz con Pollo (Chicken with Rice)

Makes 4 servings
Preparation Time: 15 minutes; 40 minutes to cook

- 1 tablespoon butter
- 1 tablespoon oil
- 1 3-pound broiler-fryer chicken, cut in serving pieces
- 1 medium-size onion, chopped
- 1 1-pound can tomatoes with juice, cut up
- 1½ cups chicken broth
- 2 small cloves garlic, pressed
- 1 teaspoon salt
- ¼ teaspoon ground black pepper
- 1 teaspoon lemon juice
- ½ teaspoon granulated sugar
- ¼ teaspoon powdered saffron or ground turmeric
- 1 bay leaf
- 1 cup uncooked white rice
- 1 10-ounce package frozen peas

Heat butter and oil in large skillet with cover over medium heat. Brown chicken, skin-side-down. Turn chicken; add onion; brown. Remove chicken pieces. Add next 9 ingredients; bring to boil. Stir in rice; top with chicken pieces; bring to boil. Cover; simmer 15 minutes over low heat. Gently stir in peas; cook 10 minutes or until chicken and rice are tender. Remove bay leaf before serving.

Lasagne

Makes 8 to 10 servings
Preparation Time: 30 minutes; 1 hour to bake

- 2 pounds lean ground beef
- ½ cup chopped onion
- 1 clove garlic, pressed
- 1 16-ounce can tomatoes
- 1 6-ounce can tomato paste
- 1 tablespoon minced parsley
- 2 teaspoons dried oregano
- 2 teaspoons salt
- 1 teaspoon granulated sugar
- 1 teaspoon dried basil
- ⅛ teaspoon ground black pepper
- 10 lasagne noodles
- 1 egg
- 1 pound ricotta cheese
- 1 pound cottage cheese with chives
- ½ cup grated Parmesan cheese
- 1½ pounds thinly sliced mozzarella cheese

Preheat oven to 375°. Grease 9 by 13-inch baking pan. Brown beef with onion and garlic in large skillet over medium heat, stirring to break up meat. Add next 4 ingredients, 1½ teaspoons salt, sugar, basil and pepper. Simmer, uncov-

ered, 5 to 7 minutes, until thick; stirring occasionally. Cook lasagne noodles according to package directions. Beat egg in bowl; stir in ricotta cheese, cottage cheese, ¼ cup Parmesan cheese and remaining ½ teaspoon salt. Arrange half of noodles in pan. Spread with half ricotta cheese mixture. Cover with one-third Mozzarella cheese slices. Top with half of meat sauce. Repeat layers. Arrange remaining one-third mozzarella over meat sauce. Sprinkle remaining ¼ cup Parmesan cheese over top. Bake, uncovered, 40 minutes. Let stand 10 to 15 minutes before serving.

Cornish Pasties

Makes 8
Preparation Time: 45 minutes; 30 minutes to bake

- 2 cups pared, cubed potato
- 1 cup cubed rutabaga
- 1 cup chopped carrot
- 1 medium-size onion, chopped
- ¼ cup chopped parsley
- 1½ teaspoons salt
- ½ teaspoon ground black pepper
- 1 pound ground beef chuck
  Pastry
- 1 egg, lightly beaten

Preheat oven to 425°. Mix first 8 ingredients in bowl. Divide Pastry into 2 parts. Roll each to 11-inch circle on lightly floured surface. Cut in 4 equal pie-shaped pieces; moisten all edges. Spread ½ cup filling on lower third of each piece of dough; fold over; crimp edges. Make two gashes in center so steam can escape during baking. Place on baking sheet; brush with beaten egg. Bake about 30 minutes. Cool on wire rack. Serve hot or cold.

Pastry

- 2½ cups sifted flour
- ½ teaspoon salt
- ⅔ cup shortening
- 4 to 5 tablespoons ice water

Combine flour and salt in bowl. Cut in shortening until mixture resembles peas. Add water; cut into flour mixture until crumbly. Turn out on lightly floured pastry cloth; form into ball.

Turkey Breast Florentine

Makes 10 to 12 servings
Preparation Time: 1 hour; 2¼ hours to bake

    1 4 to 5-pound whole turkey breast, boned
    1 tablespoon salt
    ½ teaspoon ground white pepper
       Florentine Filling
    3 tablespoons butter, melted
    ⅓ cup dry white wine
    10 to 12 medium-size sweet potatoes or yams
       Pan Gravy

Preheat oven to 450°. Rub turkey breast with salt and pepper. Skewer open edges together in 3 or 4 places making sure to attach skin of one side to skin of other side. Place skewered-end-down on cutting board. Cut turkey in 6 to 8 ½-inch thick crosswise slices, but don't cut completely through. Stuff Florentine Filling into turkey slits. Brush entire breast with melted butter. Place skin-side-up in 9 by 13-inch baking pan. Pour wine in bottom of pan; cover tightly with foil. Bake 1 hour. Reduce heat to 350°; loosely tent foil over turkey breast. Arrange potatoes on oven rack; bake 1 hour or until turkey and potatoes are tender. Remove from pan; place on platter; keep warm while preparing pan gravy. Serve turkey slices with pan gravy.

Florentine Filling

    ¼ cup butter
    ½ cup thinly sliced green onion
    2 10-ounce packages frozen chopped spinach, cooked, well-drained
    1 teaspoon poultry seasoning
    ¼ cup dry bread crumbs
    1 3-ounce package cream cheese, room temperature
    ¼ cup grated Parmesan cheese
    2 tablespoons lemon juice
    1 egg, lightly beaten

Mix all ingredients in bowl.

Pan Gravy

Makes 2 cups

    ¼ cup pan drippings
    ¼ cup flour
    ⅛ teaspoon poultry seasoning
       Turkey juices
       Chicken broth

Pour pan drippings into measuring cup. Leave crusty brown particles in roasting pan. Add butter or margarine to measure ¼ cup. Pour in roasting pan. Stir in flour and poultry season-ing. Cook over low heat, stirring constantly, until bubbly. Pour into a 2-quart saucepan. Measure turkey juices that accumulate on platter; add enough chicken broth to measure 2 cups. Add to saucepan; cook over medium heat, stirring constantly, until mixture comes to boil, 3 to 5 minutes. Serve hot.

Creamed Turkey with Popovers

Makes 8 servings
Preparation Time: 1½ hours

    ½ cup thin celery sticks, 1-inch
    ¾ cup sliced mushrooms
    ⅓ cup thin green pepper strips
    3 tablespoons minced onion
    ¼ cup butter
    3 tablespoons flour
    3 cups milk
    ¾ teaspoon poultry seasoning
    ½ teaspoon salt
    ¼ teaspoon ground white pepper
    2 tablespoons chopped pimiento, drained
    3 cups diced cooked white turkey meat
    3 tablespoons Madeira wine
    8 Popovers

Sauté first 4 ingredients in butter in saucepan over medium heat 2 minutes. Add flour; sauté 3 minutes. Add milk; stirring constantly. Add next 4 ingredients; cook over low heat 3 to 4 minutes. Add turkey and wine. Heat through. Serve in 8 Popovers.

Popovers

    3 eggs
    1 cup milk
    1 tablespoon butter or margarine, melted
    1 cup flour
    ¾ teaspoon salt
    ½ teaspoon granulated sugar

Preheat oven to 375°. Generously grease 8 5-ounce custard cups; place 4 along each long edge of jelly roll pan. Set in oven 5 minutes while mixing batter. Beat eggs in bowl until light and fluffy using hand mixer or whisk. Add milk and butter; mix well. Combine dry ingredients; add to milk mixture; beat until smooth. Pour batter evenly into custard cups using about ¼ cup for each custard cup. (Cups should be about ⅓ full.) Bake 50 minutes. Cut slit in side of each popover with sharp knife so steam can escape. Bake 10 minutes; immediately remove popovers from custard cups. Cut off tops and fill.

Turkey Breast Florentine, this page
Creamed Turkey with Popovers, this page

Turkey in Popovers—Variations

Variations
Creamed Turkey with Vegetables
Reduce turkey to 1½ cups. Add 1½ cups cooked and drained vegetables such as peas or mixed vegetables.

Creamed Turkey and Ham
Reduce turkey to 1½ cups. Add 1½ cups chopped cooked ham.

Creamed Turkey and Shrimp
Reduce turkey to 1½ cups. Add 1½ cups cooked shrimp.

Note: Diced cooked white chicken meat may be substituted for the turkey. Three whole chicken breasts (about 10 ounces each) when cooked will yield about 3 cups chopped cooked chicken.

Baked Chicken with Wild Rice

Makes 10 to 12 servings
Preparation Time: 20 minutes; 1 hour 10 minutes to bake

- 6 whole large chicken breasts, split
- 3 tablespoons butter
- 1 tablespoon lemon juice
- 2 teaspoons salt
- 1 teaspoon paprika
- ¼ teaspoon ground black pepper
- 1 pound mushrooms, sliced
- 1 cup chopped onion
- 1 cup thinly sliced celery
- 3½ cups hot chicken broth
- 1¼ cups long grain white rice mixed with ¼ cup wild rice
  Minced parsley

Preheat oven to 350°. Grease 9 by 13-inch baking pan. Sauté chicken breasts in butter in large skillet over medium heat until golden on both sides. Remove chicken; sprinkle with lemon juice. Combine salt, paprika and pepper. Sprinkle over chicken. Sauté mushrooms, onion and celery in pan drippings until onion is translucent. Add broth; bring to boil. Stir in rice; bring to boil. Pour into pan; cover tightly with foil; bake 30 minutes. Add chicken; cover; bake 30 minutes. Uncover; bake 10 minutes or until rice is done and liquid is absorbed. Garnish with minced parsley.

Sophie's Pita Pie

Makes 10 to 12 servings
Preparation Time: 1 hour 10 minutes; 50 minutes to bake

- 1 pound phyllo dough, thawed
- 1½ cups butter, melted
  Meat Filling
  Spinach Filling

Preheat oven to 350°. Grease 9 by 13-inch baking pan. Place 1 sheet of phyllo in pan. Brush entire phyllo sheet lightly with melted butter. Fold edges of dough inside to fit pan. Repeat with ½ of filo sheets, brushing each with melted butter. Top with Meat Filling; top with Spinach Filling. Top with remaining phyllo sheets, brushing each with melted butter and folding in edges to fit pan. Brush top sheet generously with butter. Chill 20 minutes. Score in 12 pieces (each about 3-inches square) with sharp knife cutting only through 4 sheets of dough. Bake 35 to 40 minutes. Let stand 10 minutes before cutting completely and serving.

Meat Filling

- 1½ pounds ground beef chuck
- ½ cup chopped onion
- 1 clove garlic, pressed
- 1 egg, lightly beaten
- ¼ cup chopped parsley
- 1 teaspoon dried dillweed
- ½ teaspoon salt
- ¼ teaspoon ground black pepper

Brown meat, onion and garlic in large skillet, stirring to break up meat. Remove from heat; cool slightly. Stir in remaining ingredients.

Spinach Filling

- 2 tablespoons salt
- 1½ pounds fresh spinach, washed, chopped, drained
- 3 cups thinly sliced onion
- 2 tablespoons olive oil
- ½ cup chopped parsley
- 1 teaspoon dried dillweed
- ½ teaspoon ground black pepper
- 2 cups crumbled feta cheese
- 3 tablespoons grated Parmesan cheese
- 6 eggs, lightly beaten

Sprinkle salt over spinach in colander; let stand 30 minutes. Squeeze out all excess water. Sauté onion in oil in skillet over medium heat until onion is translucent. Stir in spinach, parsley, dillweed and pepper; cook 1 minute. Remove from heat; stir in cheeses. Blend in eggs.

Chicken Crab Meat Casserole

Makes 8 to 10 servings
Preparation Time: 30 minutes; 30 minutes to bake

- ½ pound mushrooms, sliced, *or* 1 8-ounce can sliced mushrooms, drained
- ½ cup thinly sliced green onion
- ¼ cup butter
- 2 tablespoons flour
- 3 cups milk
- 2 cups shredded Swiss cheese, lightly packed
- 2 cups elbow macaroni, cooked, drained
- 1 7-ounce package frozen crab meat, drained, flaked
- 1½ cups diced cooked chicken *or* turkey
- 2 hard-cooked eggs, chopped
- ½ cup thinly sliced pimiento-stuffed olives
- ¼ cup diced pimiento, drained
- 1 teaspoon salt
- 1 teaspoon Worcestershire sauce
- ½ cup slivered almonds, toasted

Preheat oven to 350°. Grease 9 by 13-inch baking dish. Sauté mushrooms and green onion in butter in 3-quart saucepan over medium heat 2 to 3 minutes. Add flour; cook, stirring 2 minutes. Stir in milk; cook, stirring until slightly thickened. Remove from heat. Stir in next 9 ingredients; pour in pan. Top with almonds; bake 30 minutes.

Chili Chicken

Makes 8 to 10 servings
Preparation Time: 30 minutes; chill overnight; 2 hours to bake

- 2 3-pound broiler-fryer chickens, cut in serving pieces
- 1 tablespoon salt
- 2 16-ounce cans sliced stewed tomatoes
- 1 16-ounce can tomato sauce
- 2 cloves garlic, minced
- 2 tablespoons wine vinegar
- 4 teaspoons chili powder
- 4 15-ounce cans red kidney beans, undrained
- 3 cups diagonally sliced celery
- 3 medium-size onions, sliced
- 2 small green peppers, cored, diced

Sprinkle chicken with 1 teaspoon salt in large pan. Mix next 5 ingredients and remaining 2 teaspoons salt in bowl. Stir in remaining ingredients; pour over chicken. Cover; chill overnight. Preheat oven to 350°. Place vegetable and chicken pieces, skin-side-down in large shallow baking pan or 2 9 by 13-inch baking pans. Bake 1 hour; turn chicken pieces; bake 1 hour.

Moussaka

Makes 9 servings
Preparation Time: 40 minutes; 55 minutes to bake

- Olive oil
- 4 teaspoons salt
- 2 1½-pounds eggplants, partially peeled, cut lengthwise in ¼-inch slices
- Flour for coating
- ⅓ cup olive oil
- 2 pounds ground beef chuck *or* lamb
- 2 medium-size onions, thinly sliced
- 1 clove garlic, minced
- ½ cup water
- ½ cup dry red wine
- 1 8-ounce can tomato sauce
- ½ cup minced parsley
- ¼ teaspoon ground black pepper
- 2 tablespoons bread crumbs
- ½ cup grated Parmesan cheese

Preheat oven to 350°. Brush jelly roll pan with olive oil. Grease 9 by 13-inch baking pan. Sprinkle 2 teaspoons salt on eggplant in colander; let stand 20 minutes. Rinse off salt; lightly squeeze slices to remove excess water. Dip in flour to coat lightly. Brush eggplant slices on both sides with some of ⅓ cup olive oil. Place in jelly roll pan; broil 5 minutes on each side or until golden. Brown meat, onion and garlic in 10-inch skillet, stirring to break up meat. Add next 5 ingredients and remaining 2 teaspoons salt. Remove from heat. Stir in bread crumbs and cheese. Arrange one-third of eggplant slices on bottom of baking pan. Cover with one-third of meat. Repeat layering 2 more times, ending with meat. Top with Cream Sauce; bake 45 to 55 minutes. Let stand 10 minutes before cutting into squares.

Cream Sauce

- 6 tablespoons butter
- 4 tablespoons cornstarch
- 3 cups cold milk
- Dash salt
- 3 eggs
- Dash nutmeg

Melt butter in a 2-quart saucepan. Dissolve cornstarch in milk. Add to butter. Cook and stir until thickened, about 15 minutes. Stir in salt. Remove from heat. Cool slightly. Beat eggs well. Add about ½ cup of the hot milk mixture into eggs. Blend egg mixture and nutmeg slowly into hot milk mixture; mix well.

Seafood Newburg Crêpes

Makes 12 servings
Preparation Time: 30 minutes; 25 minutes to bake

½ cup butter
6 tablespoons flour
2 cups half-and-half
1 cup milk
½ cup dry sherry
2 cups shredded brick cheese, lightly packed
1½ pounds fresh *or* frozen small shrimp, thawed
12 ounces frozen scallops, thawed, sliced
1 pound mushrooms, sliced
2 tablespoons chopped pimiento, drained
2 tablespoons minced parsley
1 teaspoon Worcestershire sauce
2 teaspoons salt
½ teaspoon paprika
⅛ teaspoon cayenne pepper
24 Crêpes (see page 29)
Paprika

Preheat oven to 350°. Melt 6 tablespoons butter in 2-quart saucepan over medium heat. Stir in flour. Cook, stirring constantly, until smooth and bubbly. Add half and half and milk; heat to boiling, stirring constantly. Boil 1 minute. Add sherry and 1 cup cheese. Stir over low heat until cheese melts. Set aside. Sauté shrimp, scallops and mushrooms in remaining 2 tablespoons butter in skillet. Remove from heat. Stir in next 6 ingredients and 1½ cups cream sauce. Place about ¼ cup seafood mixture down center of each of 24 Crêpes; fold sides over to enclose filling. Spread ½ cup cream sauce evenly over bottom of 2 9 by 13-inch baking pans. Place Crêpes seam-side-down in pans. Pour remaining sauce over center of Crêpes; cover; bake 25 minutes. Uncover; sprinkle cheese evenly over center of each Crêpe. Bake 2 minutes or until cheese melts. Sprinkle with paprika. Serve immediately.

Aloha Chicken

Makes 10 to 12 servings
Preparation Time: 30 minutes; 55 minutes to bake

½ cup butter
1 14½-ounce can sliced pineapple, drained, reserve liquid
4 medium-size onions, sliced
½ cup flour
2 teaspoons salt
½ teaspoon ground white pepper
5 large whole chicken breasts, split
1 6-ounce can pineapple juice
4 teaspoons instant chicken bouillon granules
⅛ teaspoon ground white pepper
1 pound large macaroni shells
3 10-ounce packages frozen French-style green beans, thawed
4 cups broccoli flowerets
1 8-ounce can corn, drained
1 cup chopped red pepper *or* ¼ cup chopped pimiento, drained

Preheat oven to 375°. Melt 2 tablespoons butter in large skillet over medium heat. Sauté pineapple slices lightly on both sides, adding 2 tablespoons butter, if necessary. Remove; set aside. Add 2 tablespoons butter; sauté onion until translucent. Remove; set aside. Mix flour, salt and ½ teaspoon pepper in pie pan. Dip chicken breasts lightly in flour on both sides. Add 2 tablespoons butter to skillet; sauté chicken breasts over medium heat 10 minutes on each side. Arrange chicken, skin-side-down in large baking dish or 2 9 by 13-inch baking pans. Pour pineapple juice in 4-cup measure; add enough water to measure 3½ cups. Stir in bouillon granules and ⅛ teaspoon pepper. Pour into skillet. Bring to boil. Pour over chicken. Arrange onion on top and around chicken. Bake 25 minutes. Cook macaroni shells in boiling salted water in large kettle 6 minutes; drain; set aside. Remove chicken from pan; set aside. Put beans, broccoli, corn, macaroni shells and red pepper in baking pan. Arrange chicken breasts skin-side-up over vegetables. Top with sautéed pineapple slices. Bake 30 minutes.

Seafood Newburg Crêpes, this page

Index

BRUNCH & LUNCH
Asparagus Quiche, 31
Best-Ever Beef 'n Biscuits, 31
Broccoli Noodle Soufflé, 31
Brunch Benedict, 28
Cheese Blintzes, 28
Chicken Divan Crêpes, 28
Florentine Crêpes, 29
Fruited Chicken Mélange, 29
Gazpacho Macaroni Salad, 31
Hot Turkey Salad, 32
Reuben Casserole, 32
Sunnyside Skillet, 32
Trio Cheese Bake, 32

CASSEROLES — MEAT
Bacon Bean Bake, 21
Bavarian Supper, 16
Beef Brisket, 15
Biscuit Beef Pie, 18
Creole Beef Stew, 20
Garbanzo Lamb Stew, 20
German-Style Salad with
    Frankfurters, 18
Ham with Yams, 15
Lamb Celery Espagnole, 16
Meat Loaf Succotash, 21
Moussaka, 16
New England Boiled Dinner,
    18
Old World Casserole, 21
Oven-Barbecued Drumsticks,
    20
Parmesan Chicken, 15
Pork Chops Orient, 21
Pork Steaks Rio Grande, 21
Pot Roast in Foil, 20
Potato Pork Casserole, 18
Salisbury Steak Dinner, 17
Shepherd's Beef Pie, 17
Stuffed Cabbage, 16
Stuffed Green Peppers, 17
Taco Casserole, 15

CASSEROLES — MEATLESS
Asparagus-Potato Scallop, 11
Creamy Cheese Confetti, 11
Deviled Egg Casserole, 12
Eggplant Parmigiana, 11
Herb Cheese Casserole, 13
Layered Casserole, 12
Mediterranean Eggplant, 12
Spinach Squares, 12
Spinach Strudel, 13
Tabbouleh Salad, 13
Vegetarian Pizza, 11

CHEESE & EGGS
Athenian Omelet, 25
Autumn Apple Scramble, 24
Berry Yogurt Omelet, 22
Chicken Liver Omelet, 27
Deluxe Denver Combo, 22
Eggs Bechamel, 24

Eggs Rancheros, 24
Frozen Cheese Soufflé, 25
Hoppel Poppel, 25
Lunch for Two, 24
Potato Omelet, 22
Quiche Lorraine, 27
Skillet Scramble, 27
Welsh Rarebit, 25
Zucchini Bake, 22
Zucchini Frittata, 27

ENTERTAINING
Aloha Chicken, 63
Baked Chicken with Wild
    Rice, 60
Chicken Crab Meat Casserole,
    61
Chili Chicken, 61
Creamed Turkey with
    Popovers, 59
Lasagne, 57
Moussaka, 61
Seafood Newberg Crêpes, 63
Sophie's Pita Pie, 60
Turkey Breast Florentine, 59

FISH & SEAFOOD
Baked Fillet Swirls, 49
Captain's Crab Meat, 50
Cheese-Topped Tuna, 50
Cioppino, 52
Crab Soufflé, 49
Creamy Crab Quiche, 49
Fish Stew Marinara, 50
Salmon Casserole, 49
Salmon Rarebit, 52
Shrimp Foo Yung, 52
Tuna Scallop, 52

HOMESTYLE
Broccoli Pasta, 9
Cheese-Filled Meatballs, 9
Cheese 'n Ham Strata, 9
Chicken Lasagne, 8
Chicken Napoli, 6
Chili con Carne, 9
Homestyle Macaroni and
    Cheese, 8
Martha's Pizza Pie, 6
Mexi-Grande Pie, 6
Roman Rice Pie, 8

INTERNATIONAL
Arroz con Pollo (Chicken with
    Rice), 57
Beef Enchiladas, 56
Beef Steefatho, 56
Chicken Provençale, 54
Cornish Pasties, 57
Deep-Dish Pizza, 56
Hot Taco Salad, 53
Hungarian Goulash, 53
Lasagne, 57
Mexicali Corn Pie, 53

Paella, 54
Salonika Lamb in Foil, 54
Veal Scallopini, 53

LEFTOVERS
Beef Tabbouleh, 44
Cauliflower Frenchette, 41
Cheddar Crust Meat Pies, 43
Chicken Jambalaya Salad, 40
Curried Turkey, 40
Easy Beef Stroganoff, 40
Farm-Style Beef Hash, 40
Ham Supreme, 44
Jiffy Turkey Casserole, 40
Meat Medley Salad, 44
No-Fuss Skillet, 41
One-Pot Pasta, 43
Pasta Bolognese, 43
Pireaus Pilaf, 43
Rice Potpourri, 41
Tamale Pie, 41
Turkey Tetrazzini, 44

LOW CALORIE
Chicken Ratatouille, 45
Continental Chicken, 47
Fish Fiesta, 47
Hong Kong Stir-Fry, 47
Savory Cube Steaks, 45
Shrimp Creole, 48
Skillet Supper, 48
Tarragon Stuffed Peppers, 45
Tasty Tuna Salad, 45
Turkey Fruit Salad, 48
Veal Italiano, 48
Vegetable Chicken Chop
    Suey, 47

SKILLET
Anchovy Pot Roast, 36
Basque-Style Veal Skillet, 38
Beef Zucchini Skillet, 33
Chicken Noodle Skillet
    Dinner, 36
Country-Style Chicken, 36
Dilled Beef Stew Skillet, 36
15-Minute Skillet Casserole,
    34
Garden Skillet Stew, 38
Lamb Shank Pilaf, 33
One-Pot Veal Parmigiana, 33
Pork-Cauliflower Stew, 37
Pork Chops Frijoles, 37
Pork Chops Oregano, 34
Pork Hocks, 37
Pot Luck Skillet Supper, 33
Short Ribs and Dumplings,
    37
Skillet Meat Loaf, 34
Spicy Sausage Serenade, 34
Sweet-Sour Skillet, 34
30-Minute Skillet Supper, 38
Yankee Pot Roast, 38